EVANGELISM BY FIRE

Igniting Your Passion for the Lost

REINHARD BONNKE

EVANGELISM by FIRE

Igniting Your Passion for the Lost

Unless otherwise indicated, all Scripture quotations are taken from the *New King James Version* of the Bible, copyright © 1982 by Thomas Nelson, Inc., Nashville, Tennessee. Other quotations, as noted, are from *King James Version* of the Bible; and from *The Holy Bible, New International Version (NIV)*, copyright © 1978 by the International Bible Society and used by permission of Zondervan Bible Publishers.

Cover design by Karl-Heinz Schablowski
Literary production by Rev. George Canty
Editing by Ruth M. Wilson

ISBN 1-882729-00-5

Printed in the United States of America

A Reinhard Bonnke Ministries, Inc. Publication

DEDICATION

*I dedicate this book
to all the fellow-fishers of men
of the ministry of "Christ for all Nations"
who helped me to throw out the Gospel net
over Africa and the world
and
in particular, to
Pastor Michael T. Kolisang from Lesotho,
Rev. Peter Vandenberg from Zimbabwe, and
Evangelist Suzette Hattingh from Germany*

Table of Contents

Part V: In Practice

EVANGELISM
BY
FIRE

REVIVAL NO COINCIDENCE

Twenty-five years ago, as a young missionary in Africa, I sometimes preached to five people. My opportunity to see the impact of the glorious Gospel presented in the "proven" tradition of foreign missions had come. *But five people?* Beyond our mission there were 450 million souls in Africa, most of whom were ignorant of salvation through Jesus Christ. Yes, they could all be evangelized by the way we were tackling it, but only if they obliged us by staying alive for about 5000 years!

However, small audiences did not dismay us. Revival could come and save us a lot of trouble. God could rouse Himself to battle. This hope kept us patient and starry-eyed, for had not our spiritual great grandfathers banked upon this with unquestioning faith?

AN UNPREACHED GOSPEL IS USELESS

Later, I began questioning this idea. It struck me that *the Gospel is not good news to people who don't hear it—that an unpreached Gospel is no Gospel at all.* Another small ray of illumination penetrated my heart: In the New Testament we never read about God going forth on His own, but that, *"They* went out and preached everywhere, the Lord working with *them"* (Mark 16:20, emphasis mine). God acted when they acted. Smith Wigglesworth said, "The Acts of the Apostles was written because the Apostles acted!"

"For since in the wisdom of God the world through its wisdom did not know him, God was pleased through the foolishness of what was preached to save those who believe." (1 Cor. 1:21 NIV)

So, He was waiting for us, and—I couldn't get away from it—that included me.

I set up a Bible correspondence course, and 50,000 people enrolled. So many! Like a periscope from a submarine, it revealed that I was submerged in an ocean of salvation-hungry humanity. In addition, a vision followed me. Night after night I saw the entire African continent, washed in the Blood of Jesus, country after country.

Wait for revival? We had! The waiting had been done, thoroughly and patiently, through a hundred long years of earnest prayer. Surely God must answer now?

Yet, one more fact faced me,—there had never been revival without aggressive evangelism. So, on a seemingly wild impulse, which proved to be of God, I booked a 10,000 seat stadium for a campaign with a church of 40 members—10,000 people came! The first ripe wheat. For the first time I witnessed thousands running forward to respond to the call of salvation. God opened my eyes and I actually saw an invisible, mighty wave of Holy Spirit-power arrive in the stadium. A mass baptism in the Holy Spirit, accompanied by many healing miracles, took place. I wept like a boy and vowed to the Lord that in obedience I would move across all of Africa to bring the vision to pass. I reasoned that if God can do that to 10,000 people, He could do it to 450 million.

What we are seeing God do today in Africa is breathtaking. Following the footsteps of giants, we reap with joy where they had sown in tears. We came to Bukavu, first visited by missionary C.T. Studd, and still remote in the rain forests of Zaire. There we saw 70,000 people respond to the call of God's love. David Livingstone prophesied that where he hardly saw a convert, later there would be thousands. So it was.   At Blantyre, Malawi, named after the town in Scotland where Livingstone was born, several hundred thousand responded to the call of salvation.

PULLING THE REVIVAL-TRIGGER

Today, witchcraft, occultism and evil make the Gospel as vital as a gun in a snake pit. The devil is on the run as Jesus sets the captives free wholesale. Cool and casual Christianity will do nothing. Nations urgently need the flaming message of the Cross now, not at our leisure.

Presidents and leaders observe the miraculous benefits conferred by the Gospel upon their peoples, and welcome us personally.   In March 1990, our northerly thrust reached almost to the Sahara Desert at Ouagadougou, capital of Burkina Faso (formerly Upper Volta); a country noted for its occultism.   The President brought us into his home twice. Gatherings totalled 800,000 people in six meetings, with almost a quarter million people in the culminating service. Most of them professed Jesus Christ, including many Muslims and animists.   Similarly, in August of 1990, in the Nigerian city of Kaduna, 500,000 people gathered in a single service—a total of 1.67 million in six meetings.   The response to the power-Gospel is absolutely awesome!

Today there is a divine promise in my heart that we shall see one million souls converted in a single meeting. We are acquiring sound systems to reach crowds bigger than perhaps ever addressed before on earth by one man face to face. Arrogant presumption?   If the Crucified One is to "see the labor of His soul, and be satisfied," as Isaiah 53:11 states, dare we think in smaller terms?   Would He be "satisfied" with anything less?   Why should the servants of God plan like Lilliputians?

FLASH-FLOOD

God says, "For the earth will be filled with the knowledge of the glory of the LORD, as the waters cover the sea" (Hab. 2:14). How do the waters cover the sea? So thoroughly that there is not a single dry spot on the bottom of the sea! This clearly illustrates God's plan. The knowledge of His glory, power and salvation will be spread across the world like a flash flood. There won't be a single dry spot, no ignorant country, city, town, village, family or individual. "The whole earth is full of His glory," cried the seraphim (Isa. 6:3).

This decade must become the culmination of a century of global evangelism and revival, the consummation of the toils and tears of former generations of God's anointed. The church is a lifeboat, not a pleasure boat. Entertainers are not needed or wanted. From the captain to the cook all hands are needed on deck for soul saving. The church that does not seek the lost is "lost" itself. Some excuse themselves saying that in today's pluralistic societies the Christian half can never penetrate the other half. But was not our situation anticipated by God?

People ask, "What is God saying to the Church today?" Why is that a problem? Does God speak so inaudibly? He says nothing today that is not in His Word already. I know one thing that God is saying. If our prophets are true they will be voicing the same urgency as Jesus Christ, and echoing the same Great Commission: "Go into all the world and preach the gospel to every creature" (Mark 16:15).

EVANGELISTS SOUGHT

Evangelists? Thousands of them are in church jobs to which God never called them. It is time for the Body of Christ to boldly reaffirm the Office of Evangelist! Some pastors become angry if you ask why God has given evangelists. The fact remains forever that God's concern today, as at Calvary, is the salvation of souls. And when Jesus Christ ascended into Heaven, He established the work of evangelists within the Church to help accomplish this great work (Eph. 4:8-16).

The past holds tragedies. When doors opened, some Christian workers were found jealously guarding their monopoly as did gold miners their claim. Sometimes rivalries ruined revivals. The harvest must not go unreaped while reapers merely defend their "own" flock. Christ did not die to give people a career but to save the lost.

This is not a book of means and methods, but of spiritual principles. God will give you resourcefulness. There are as many methods as He directs. We need more imaginative approaches, rather than people doing things by "tried and proved" methods—including methods I have tried and proved. Methods which have made little impact in the past are not likely to produce an impact now. Plodding along mechanically might be called faithfulness, but our primary concern in evangelism is effectiveness, not a twisted type of faithfulness.

During my years as an evangelist and missionary I have discovered a number of limiting factors hindering the Gospel. Although I do not address these directly in this book, I know from experience that many of the "traditional and accepted" methods of evangelism have remained unchanged for generations. Others are doctrines and sentiments which tell us to "leave it all to God." Some insist God's way is revival, but they fail to carry out the Great Commission in the meantime. Some think that if people are to be saved, they will be saved anyway.

Suppose such doctrines are wrong! What an awful risk— to rest the eternal destiny of souls upon a controversial interpretation of Scripture or turn of a Greek verb. One can be dead right, but dead nonetheless! We dare not neglect the task of evangelism. I would rather use a method despised by man but approved by God, than a method approved by man which gets no results.

It is for this reason I make no apology for this book. I am not writing to be approved by man. I am writing to share God's anointing on all those who are ready to step out in faith. The temperature of this book runs hot—very hot. Its flames will scorch. Some who read these pages would do well to take out fire insurance, for I guarantee many old concepts will be set to the torch.

My message is not one-sided, but it does come from a singleness of heart. I hammer away at the Great Commission, for I know it cannot be overemphasized. I cry to God day and night for greater effectiveness in winning our generation for Him. EVANGELISM BY FIRE is the only feasible solution.

I constantly scan the horizons for other anointed men and women who may take up this challenge of the Word of God for Holy Spirit evangelism. I believe the best is yet to be. The time is coming soon when the whole world will resound with the praises of our God and Savior. In all nations and in every language, the day is almost here when every tongue will confess that "Jesus Christ is Lord, to the glory of God the Father" (Phil. 2:11).

This book is filled with the things God has taught me, and allowed me to experience over the years. I'm writing for one reason alone—to inspire others to "do the work of an evangelist" (2 Tim:4:5). I have laid out the principles necessary for any Holy Spirit ministry. Read it, not to discover how I operate in my evangelism crusades, but to discover how God operates through anyone willing to follow His plan.

THE IMMENSE PRIVILEGE

The angel who appeared to Cornelius in Acts 10 was not allowed to mention the name of Jesus, or to speak about salvation to the man. That high and holy privilege was (and is) reserved for men—people like you and me. All the angel was allowed to say was, "Now send men to Joppa, and send for Simon whose surname is Peter" (Acts 10:5). This mighty seraphim from deep heaven had to bow to Peter's higher privilege. It pleases God to call and to send people like you and me.

It has always been this way. God used four evangelists—Matthew, Mark, Luke and John—to write down the story of the Gospel of Jesus Christ. Such a pattern is linked, in my mind, to the four men in Old Testament times who carried the Ark of the Covenant. Carriers of the Gospel change from generation to generation, but the Gospel remains the same. Now we are here, and today it is our turn. God has called you and me. The Gospel needs to be taken to the ends of the earth. This is the Great Commission of the Lord to us—and the King's business requires haste.

HOW BIG IS HELL?

These chapters are written because I do not believe that God's plans call for hell to be bigger than heaven. Although Scripture speaks about "many" who are on their way to eternal destruction (Matt. 7:13), these same people must be intercepted by men and women preaching the original Gospel. Provision has been made to bring "many sons to glory" (Heb. 2:10); and, praise God, Revelation 7:9 speaks of a successful conclusion.

Jesus instructed, "Go . . . and make disciples of all the nations" (Matt. 28:19). There is no alternate plan in case the

Gospel fails because *it won't!* More people are being saved, healed and baptized into the Holy Spirit today than ever before in man's history. The tempo is increasing, leading to but one conclusion: **Jesus is coming soon.**

We are not called to go into a battle with the outcome yet to be decided. The battle was won at Calvary. Jesus commanded the disciples: "Pray the Lord of the harvest to send out laborers" (Matt. 9:38), and added, "Go!" He still says it. It is a transferred mandate.

Revival comes from God, yes, but when? When we repent of our plain disobedience and return to the basic task—Evangelism. Every single church activity should relate to turning the world back to God. Why are we waiting? "Rescue the perishing," or we'll need rescuing ourselves.

Part I
The Need

Chapter 1

WHEN ARSON IS NOT A CRIME!

God sets driftwood on fire. Dry old sticks can burn for God, just like Moses' bush did! Hallelujah!

John the Baptist stood in the cold waters of Jordan, baptizing, but Jesus the Baptizer stands in a river of liquid fire.

I don't pray, "Let me burn out for Thee, dear Lord." I don't want to be an ash heap. The amazing feature of the bush was that it didn't burn out. Too many of the Lord's servants are burning out. The cause of that is some other kind of fire. I say instead, "Let me burn on for Thee, dear Lord." The altar flame should never go out.

Without fire, there is no Gospel. The New Testament begins with fire. The first thing said about Christ by His first witness concerned fire. John the Baptist, himself a "burning and shining light" declared:

"He will baptize you with the Holy Spirit and fire. His winnowing fan is in His hand, and He will thoroughly clean out His threshing floor, and gather His wheat into the barn; but He will burn up the chaff with unquenchable fire." (Matt. 3:11-12)

John the baptizer introduced Jesus the Baptizer, the Baptizer with a vast difference. John used water, a physical element, but Christ was to use a spiritual element, holy fire. Water and fire—what a contrast! Not that John the Baptist had a watery religion (though there is plenty of that around, often combined with ice!). John the Baptist stood in the cold waters of Jordan, baptizing, but Jesus the Baptizer stands in a river of liquid Fire.

The notable work of John was baptism. He announced the notable work of Jesus as baptism also. Baptism is the Lord's present great work. Jesus the Baptizer—in the Holy Spirit. This is Christ's major experience for you after you become a born-again believer.

INCENDIARISTS

Fire is the ensign of the Gospel, the sign of the Son of Man. Only Jesus baptizes in fire.

The Gospel is a fire lighter. The Holy Spirit is not given just to help you preach eloquent sermons. He is to put a flame into human hearts. Unless Christ sets you alight, you can bring no fire to earth. "Without Me, you can do nothing," said the Lord (John 15:5). Jesus instructed the disciples not to do anything until they were to receive "power from on high" (Luke 24:49). When that power came, the Spirit revealed Himself as tongues of flame sitting upon each one of them.

Jesus previously had sent the disciples out in pairs (Luke 10:1). It reminds me of Samson sending foxes out two by two, as the animals carried torches for an arson raid on the enemy's corn shocks and vineyards (Judges 15). The disciples also were sent out two by two, carriers of the divine torch, incendiaries for God, scorching the devil's territories with the fire Gospel. They were new Elijahs bringing fire from heaven.

Until the fire falls, evangelism and church activities can be very routine and unexciting. Pulpit essays, homilies, moralizing or preaching about how you think the economy of the country should be run—all that is glacial work. No divine spark brings combustion to ice. No one goes home ignited. In contrast, the two who listened to Jesus on the Emmaus road went home with warmed hearts. I am sure He didn't talk politics to them, nor offer suggestions and advice. That wouldn't make their hearts burn. Jesus came "to send fire on the earth" (Luke 12:49). The mission of Jesus is not a holiday picnic—Satan is determined it will not be. He is a destroyer. The Lord sends out His servants with a warning of physical dangers. "And do not fear those who kill the body but are not able to kill the soul. But rather fear Him who is able to destroy both soul and body in hell" (Matt 10:28). What is mere physical hurt, compared to a life ablaze with the joy and zest of Jesus? What is bodily danger compared to the crown of life or to the wonderful work He gives us to do? "Heal the sick, cleanse the lepers, raise the dead, cast out demons. Freely you have received, freely give" (Matt. 10:8).

THE SIGN OF THE SON OF MAN

Fire is the ensign of the Gospel, the sign of the Son of Man. Only Jesus baptizes in fire. When we see such baptisms, that is the evidence that He, and nobody else, is at work. It is the identifying hallmark of His activity and of the true outburst of Christian faith. Put your hand on such activities, and you will feel the heat. The prophet Elijah made the same point— "The God who answers by fire, He is God" (1 Kings 18:24). Only one God does that. Elijah was sure that Baal was incapable of it.

Faith-chilling items have nothing to do with the Christ of Pentecost. Whatever He touches catches fire.

What does your spiritual thermometer read? Does it even register? Are you chilled? Are there cold altars in the Church? Worship without warmth? Doctrines heated only by friction? There are theologies and teachings as fireproof as asbestos. There are religious books that only provide heat if put in a bonfire. Such faith-chilling items have nothing to do with the Christ of Pentecost. Whatever He touches catches fire. Jesus melts the ice. Some church efforts to whip up a little enthusiasm are, spiritually, like rubbing two sticks together.

DUMMY AMMUNITION

The fire of God is special—unique. Only the fire of God was allowed on the altar of Moses, not fire produced by any human means. Nadab and Abihu made fire themselves and lit their incense with it. It was labelled "profane fire." Divine fire gushed from the tabernacle, swallowing up the false fire and bringing about the deaths of the rebel priests (Lev. 10:1-2).

Today, we have profane fire being offered. Strange gospels which are not Gospel at all, but theologies of unbelief, the thoughts of men and their philosophies, criticisms and theories. They bear no trace of the glory-heat from heaven. Nothing in them produces any combustion except controversy.

What lies behind all this is something which my friend Paul C. Schoch pointed out to me. He quoted Matthew 16:23, where Jesus addressed Satan when speaking to the Apostle Peter:

> "Get behind Me, Satan! You are an offense to Me, for you are not mindful of the things of God, but the things of men."

Thoughts exist on two opposing levels. There are the thoughts of God and the thoughts of men. The high and the low, as God said in Isaiah 55:8-9. Satan thinks as men think. The fact is, Satan simply cannot grasp God's outlook at all. That is strange when you remember that he was originally Lucifer, a throne angel of God. Jesus bruised the serpent's head, and I think He inflicted some kind of brain damage upon the devil! He is disoriented. Once Satan was full of wisdom, but today that prince of the power of the air is baffled by what God is doing, and especially by what the Lord did at the Cross. This type of confusion is brought on by sin.

Satan thinks as men think. This means that men think as the devil thinks. They, too, find the Cross foolishness and cannot grasp the things of God, as the Apostle Paul remarked. Paul also could not "see" it at first. Cold fury against the believers ate away in his heart. He was a "dragon man," breathing out threats and slaughter. Full of zeal, his brain was full of clever unbelief. Scales fell from his eyes, though, when he believed.

I wonder if hell would like to send espionage agents into the Kingdom of God, just to see what secrets are there? The demons wouldn't understand these secrets, anyway. Hell is completely baffled. To Satan, Christ's sacrifice is a deep-rooted plot devised by God for His own advantage. The devil devours others. That is his evil nature.

If we were to fight the devil on the level of human thought, we must remember that he thinks as men think. Satan invented a human chess game and has played this game for thousands of years. The devil anticipates our every move, and he will checkmate us ten moves ahead. Satan has experience from the time of Adam onward, and he knows every trick of human ingenuity on the board. You cannot produce faith by the wisdom of words. The devil always has a counter-statement for whatever you say.

The Gospel didn't come out of somebody's head. A university professor didn't give it to us. We have to move into the divine dimension, as there the enemy cannot follow us. The devil is no match for the mind of the Holy Spirit. If we plan, preach, witness and evangelize as men, Satan will foil us. He can handle psychology and propaganda. The answer is— move in the Spirit and preach the Gospel as it is. Then the arch-confuser becomes confused and He can't follow the game at all. The devil doesn't even know the Holy Spirit's alphabet.

We see this constantly in our Gospel crusades. We open the meetings to the Holy Spirit completely. The results are thrilling. Whole countries are challenged by the mighty power of Christ. Where false religion and doctrines of demons previously have prevailed, they are shaken and broken! No preacher could do this, no matter how popular or clever. Such success happens only when God does it His way. When He enters the field, there is a mighty victory. He can, will and *does* succeed—every time we allow Him to take over.

These breakthroughs are part of the End Time blessings the Lord promised. The Day of Pentecost continued—it did not stop at Jerusalem, but is for "the end of the earth" (Acts 1:8). I offer this challenge: let anybody begin to work on the level of the Holy Spirit, and see if he experiences anything less than the Lord's own rescue and deliverance. This kind of evangelism will break Satan's back world wide, and he will be routed. It is this holy Fire which cannot be imitated.

LIVE AMMUNITION AND "FULL STEAM AHEAD"

When a gun is loaded with blanks, the bang and recoil are the same as they would be with live ammunition. A difference can be observed in the use of live ammunition and blanks, but not in the noise.

> *Just being happy and clappy does not satisfy God's design. The Holy Spirit works for eternal purposes.*

The dummy ammunition makes no mark on the target, because it never reaches it. The real bullet can hit its mark. We are not interested in mere bang and recoil, excitement and spectacular Gospel displays, even if those draw hundreds of thousands of people. We want to see something live hit the bull's-eye. The crowds may come, but we must, by faith, let loose a true broadside of Holy Spirit fire power in order for something to be accomplished. Multitudes are born again, lives are completely changed, churches are filled, hell is plundered and heaven is populated. Hallelujah!

The fire of God is not sent just for the enjoyment of a few emotional experiences. Praise God, though, the fire of God has that glorious side effect. Holy Spirit power produces lively meetings. But just being happy and clappy does not satisfy God's design. The Holy Spirit works for eternal purposes.

I think of this when I see these now almost extinct old steam engines puffing away. These iron horses are like living creatures, breathing steam with fire in their bellies. The fireman's job is to stoke the fire and get a full head of steam going. When the steam pressure is up, the driver can do one of two things. He either can pull the whistle lever, or he can turn the lever that directs power onto the pistons. The whistle will blow off steam until there's none left, making itself heard for miles around. If power is directed onto the pistons, however, the steam can turn the wheels with far less fuss, drawing no attention to itself. The train then rolls away, carrying its load across the land. Thank God for the train whistle. It is important. But if blowing a whistle was all that steam could do, making a fire under the boiler and stoking it up wouldn't be worthwhile.

> *The proper purpose of Pentecost is to get the wheels rolling for God in every church, thereby transporting the Gospel across the face of the whole earth.*

The fire of the Holy Spirit brings power. Never mind the noise—let us apply this power to get on the move. Thunder is justified after lightning has struck. The proper purpose of Pentecost is to get the wheels rolling for God in every church, thereby transporting the Gospel across the face of the whole earth.

"Go into all the world and preach the gospel to every creature." (Mark 16:15)

The Church is a "Go" Church, not a "Sit" Church. Look outward, to where our Lord is moving across the continents. Some are looking inward, everlastingly examining their own souls, incapacitated by introspection. Jesus is saving you, don't you worry. Now start helping Him to save others. If the

Holy Spirit has come, then be up and going. He does the work, not you or me. "Woe is me if I do not preach the gospel!" (I Cor. 9:16). And woe to them to whom we fail to preach *it!*

THE CHRISTIAN AGE IS THE FIRE AGE

Let me ask a question. Why was Jesus exalted to the right hand of God? In even the greatest of commentaries, far too little is written. Christ's ascension seems to be a neglected study. Is it of such little importance? Jesus declared His ascension to be expedient (John 16:7). He told us that, unless He went to the Father, a most essential experience would never be ours. Without the Lord's ascension, we could never be baptized into the Spirit.

If baptizing into the Holy Spirit is His work, what does it mean? It means that everything to do with Him and with the Gospel should be characterized by fire. It should burn.

Look back upon all that Jesus did. John writes that His works were so many that, if they were all written, the whole world could not contain the books. So, what could there be that He did not do when He was on earth? There was one thing. It was the very thing which John the Baptist said He would do—baptize in fire and in the Holy Spirit. He didn't do that when He was on earth. Jesus came from heaven and had to return there, via the Cross and the tomb, before the final part of His mission could begin.

Nothing Jesus did on earth could be described as baptizing with the Holy Spirit and with fire. In none of His mighty works—His preaching, His teaching, His healing, or in His death and resurrection—did He baptize with the Holy Spirit. Jesus did much for His disciples. He gave them authority to carry out healing missions, but He went away without baptizing them into the Holy Spirit.

Such a baptism could not have happened until He went to the Father. Indeed, the Lord not only said it, but He emphasized it. He entered Glory to take up this brand new office, the office of the Baptizer into the Holy Spirit. This is the reason He ascended to the Father. The Old Testament knows nothing of such a baptism. It is God's "new thing." Jesus brings us many other blessings now, of course. He is our High Priest, our Advocate, our Representative. But He Himself did not name these works. He only described the sending forth of the Spirit.

After He ascended, and not before, the Spirit came and, "divided tongues, as of fire, . . . sat upon each of them" (Acts 2:3). Years before, the altars of the Tabernacle of Moses and the Temple of Solomon had been set ablaze by the pure fire from heaven. The flames in the Upper Room of Pentecost came from the same heavenly source. Jesus has all power at His command. He is in the control room.

TONGUES OF FIRE

If baptizing into the Holy Spirit is His work, what does it mean? It means that everything to do with Him and with the Gospel should be characterized by fire. It should burn. There should be fire in those who witness and work. Fire in those who preach. Fire in the Truth we preach—"Is not My word like a fire?" (Jer. 23:29). Fire in the Lord we preach—"For our God is a consuming fire." (Heb. 12:29). Fire in the power to preach—"Tongues as of fire" (Acts 2:3). Fire in the Spirit by which we preach—"The Holy Spirit and fire" (Matt. 3:11).

Now let me show you some very important concepts about God's fire:

1. All Sacrifice Must Be Consumed by Fire.

There were two sacrifices on Mount Carmel. One was per-
formed by the priests of Baal, the other by Elijah. The first
one, the sacrifice to Baal, never burned. It was fireless. The
sacrifice was there. The sacrificers were intensely earnest.
They prayed to Baal all day, and they lanced themselves with
knives to show how desperate their sincerity was. They put
everything they had into it, and yet their sacrifice brought no
fire. If the devil could have brought up a spark or two from
hell to make a blaze, Satan would have, but the altar just
stayed cold.

Fire did not fall because Elijah set up a sacrifice, either. It
came when Elijah prayed and believed. "Faith is victory."
Elijah set everything up as he should, that is true. He followed
the instructions of Moses to the letter, but no fire resulted
purely from his obedience. Faith brought the blaze.

> *God sent the
> fire on the
> sacrifice only.
> There would be
> no point in
> sending the fire
> without the
> sacrifice.*

God sent the fire on the sacrifice
only. There would be no point in
sending the fire without the sacrifice.
Armchair Christians receive no fire.
There is no such thing as an anointed
"couch-potato."   Sometimes people
pray for fire when they are not yielded
to God at all, and subsequently do
little for Him. They give up little time
or money, and render no effort.   If
they had God's fire, what would they
do with it? Sit at home and just enjoy it? The fire is not to
save us trouble in winning the world—it is to empower us to
preach the Gospel in spite of trouble.

It is the fire that matters. Laying out and setting up a
sacrifice is not enough. God won't save souls and heal the
sick until we lay our all on the altar for Him—that is true. But
our sacrifice is not *why* He does it. He performs His wonders
of salvation and healing because of His mercy and grace.

Elijah's godliness did not generate the awesome lightning that burned up everything on the altar. The fire did not come from his holiness. Your tithes and offerings cannot buy a tiny candle flame of the celestial flame. The fire of God comes, not because of our sacrifice, but because of Christ's sacrifice. Therefore, thank God, the fire is for all. Revival fire is not a reward for good people. It is God's gift. Why struggle for it? People talk about "paying the price." But it is a case of "You pay much too much for what's given freely." Fire comes by faith.

> *Armchair Christians receive no fire. There is no such thing as an anointed "couch-potato."*

2. Truth Needs to Be Fire Baptized.

We can be dead right, but dead nonetheless. We can insist on the "body of truth," but it may be a cold corpse. Jesus did not merely say, "I am the way and the truth." He said, "I am the way, the truth, *and the life*" (John 14:6 emphasis mine). God said He would put in Zion, "the shining of a flaming fire" (Isa. 4:5). Jesus testified that John the Baptist, "was the burning and shining lamp" (John 5:35). These are images of light and heat. The Gospel is a hot Gospel, no matter how much the silly world smiles at it. I do not know how to preach the "living oracles" of God (Acts 7:38), without being lively. The Gospel is to be on fire. To preach the Gospel coolly and casually would be ridiculous. One day a lady told me that there was a "demon" sitting on her, although she was a born-again Christian. I said to her, "Flies can only sit on a cold stove, and on a cold stove they can sit very long! Get the fire of the Holy Spirit into your life, and that dirty demon will not dare to touch you, lest he burn his filthy fingers." The Gospel provides its own fiery power. It is natural, therefore, for a preacher to be fired-up.

GOD'S FIRE IN JESUS

In human experience, God's fire translates into passion, the type of passion we saw in Jesus. Perhaps He wasn't only passionate in His words. When Jesus was going to Jerusalem for the last time, we read that He was walking ahead of His disciples. They saw how He urged Himself onward.

Now they were on the road, going up to Jerusalem, and Jesus was going before them; and they were amazed. And as they followed they were afraid. (Mark 10:32)

Why?—Somehow the fires in His soul were evident in the way He walked. When they arrived, Jesus saw the desecration of the temple. The disciples then had further evidence of His passionate feeling. His reaction turned Him into an awesome figure. The disciples were reminded of the words of Psalm 69:9: "Because zeal for Your house has eaten me up." But it was a love anger, not a cold fury. Jesus wasn't a frenzied fanatic. He loved His Father's house, that's all. It was his desire to see people in the temple, worshipping with freedom and happiness. But commercialism in the temple had spoiled all that. His heart overflowed like a volcano. The fire in His soul made Him cleanse the temple. His actions were frightening, and many fled from the scene because of them. The children, the blind and the lame stayed, though, and He healed them (Matt. 21:14-16).

That was what He had wanted to do, anyway, and that was the reason His anger achieved furnace heat. His indignation aimed for joy. Jesus got the children singing, "Hosanna!" This was the only occasion in Scripture where excitement about God was rebuked, the only time a hush was demanded in the courts of the Lord. The silence was demanded by the Pharisees—the praise of the Lord was drowning the tinkling of their commercial tills. Money music was muted! This was all part of the picture of the fire of the Lord.

A MUSEUM
OF MARBLE FIGURES

A burning message, and nothing but that, was supposed to be presented to the world. There don't have to be fireworks. Firebrands don't need to be hotheads. Everything about the Church, however, should reflect the warm light of God, to the very highest steeple. "And in His temple everyone says, 'Glory'" (Psalm 29:9). We read that God makes His ministers "a flame of fire" (Heb. 1:7). His people should be torches. Not only evangelists, but witnesses, ministers, church officials, leaders, workers, teachers and administrators should all glow with the Holy Spirit, like torches in a cold street. The business meeting should see Holy Spirit fire just as much as the revival meeting, perhaps even more so.

I've heard sermons that were like lectures on embalming the dead. Would such talk remind anyone of the Living Jesus? Neither Jesus, Peter nor Paul left congregations sitting like marble statues in a museum.

A fish has the same temperature as the water in which it swims. Too many Christians are like fish—they have no more warmth of spirit than the cold, unbelieving world around them. Men are warm-blooded creatures. That is the way the Lord made us. That is also the way He chose us to take the Good News—with warmth!

The Lord does not send us out because we have cool heads and dignity. Nor does He choose us because of our self-composure. He sends us out with live coals from the altar, as witnesses to the Resurrection, to testify that we have met the God of Pentecost. I've heard sermons that were like lectures on embalming the dead. Would such a talk remind anyone of the Living Jesus? Neither Jesus, Peter nor Paul left congregations sitting like marble statues in a museum.

> *A burning message, and nothing but that, was supposed to be presented to the world. There don't have to be fireworks. Firebrands don't need to be hotheads.*

Logic can be set alight and still be logic, like the logic of Isaiah or Paul, for example. Logic need not belong to the glacial period. Fire implies fervor, not ignorance. Learn, by all means, but not if it puts the fire out. Remember—radiance before cleverness. "And you shall love the Lord your God with all your heart, with all your soul, and with all your mind, and with all your strength" (Mark 12:30). The Lord wants us to have an "on fire" heart, and to radiate joy, compassion and love.

Human dignity takes on a new meaning when people are rapt in praise to God. Have you ever seen 50,000 people weeping, waving, jumping and shouting in gladness to God? What else would you expect to happen when a mother stands on our platform, testifying that her child has just been healed of congenital blindness or deafness, or perhaps of twisted limbs? I have seen these miracle testimonies so often. It is a glorious scene—the height of human experience.

It is not to our credit when we keep perfectly cool as the lame walk and the blind see. Such reserve isn't clever—it is foolish. Dance—that's more in keeping with such moments. We should take joy in the presence of the Lord! Jesus said that, at such times, even the stones would cry out (Luke 19:40).

I look at the precious men and women, black or white, many who were so sad earlier, standing in a meeting, hands pressed together in emotion or lifted in worship, eyes glistening with glad tears, faces turned up to God, lips moving in wondering thankfulness. I say to myself, "How beautiful they are!"

In such moments, I wish I was an artist. When dignity comes before our delight in God, that is a catastrophe!

If God does not touch our feelings, the devil will. How can God convict sinners and help them come to repentance unless they feel moved? How can He grant them the joy of sins forgiven, without giving them any sensation in their souls? *I believe an evangelist's job is to light a fire in the human spirit.*

Getting folks saved is more than getting their names on a dotted line. Christianity isn't a club they are joining. Salvation is spiritual surgery. What is the forgiveness which we proclaim? What sort of forgiveness did Jesus give? It was the real kind of mercy. This forgiveness made a cripple walk again, and it melted a street woman's hardness, causing her to wash His feet with tears. It was the sort of forgiveness which made people love much. It was the kind which made them do something extravagant, like throw a party as Levi did. This forgiveness caused Mary to break open a box of spikenard worth a small fortune, and Zaccheaus to give away lots of money.

The disciples were crazy with joy when they cast out devils, but Jesus said that was nothing.

> "Do not rejoice in this, that the spirits are subject to you, but rather rejoice because your names are written in heaven." In that hour Jesus rejoiced in the Spirit. (Luke 10:20-21)

Peter heard Him say those words, and he took in that lesson. Later Peter wrote this about believers:

> Whom having not seen, you love. Though now you do not see Him, yet believing, you rejoice with joy inexpressible and full of glory, receiving the end of your faith—the salvation of your souls. (1 Pet. 1:8-9)

Rejoice in undertones? Worship in whispers? Participate in silent celebrations? That is not what the word "rejoice" means in this Scripture. It means "to exult, shout, be rapturous." Try doing that without emotion, without fire!

The fire of the Holy Spirit is for real. It must flow through the Church of Jesus Christ like blood through the veins. God's people on fire, and the Church as a whole on fire, will win our lost generation for Him.

Chapter 2

THE ANTI-ANOINTED!

HOW LONG CAN THE LAST HOUR LAST?

Suppose it was your last hour! What would you be doing? What a flurry of anxious preparations there would be! But let me tell you, it *is* the last hour.

"Little children, it is the last hour . . ." (1 John 2:18). I know that it seems that this hour has lasted very long, as John wrote those words nineteen hundred years ago. But don't let that fact confuse you. Of one thing we can be certain—if it was the last hour then, it most certainly is now! If John were writing today he probably would write, "Little children, it is the last second of the last hour."

When John wrote this verse, he was watching God's clock, not ours. Its hands have not stood still. How long will God's hour last, measured by earthly time keeping methods? The one thing we know is that we *don't* know how near we are to the end. "But of that day and hour no one knows," Jesus said in Matthew 24:36. It is obvious, however, that we are much closer to the end every day. Paul saw it that way too: "Knowing the time, that now it is high time to awake out of sleep; for now our salvation is nearer than when we first believed" (Rom. 13:11).

If anybody thought they had only 60 minutes left, they would certainly not spend the time on trivialities. With the microseconds running out like fine sand in an hourglass, they would see what was really important to them. They would not go shopping for the latest fashionable hat, or run an eye down the financial columns to see how their shares were doing. Focusing on the end would put all of life into its proper perspective.

Somebody once said that most people live as if this life were a permanent arrangement. The Bible's message is that our days are "numbered"—not numberless. There is actually only time for the important things. I am thinking about the Church of Jesus Christ in particular. People often point out that life consists of a thousand details, but the minor must not outweigh the major. The Church is to concern itself with one aim—the war with Satan and the campaign for souls.

The great quality of Jesus is that He came when the Father sent Him. And the great quality about us should be that we go when Jesus sends us. "As the Father has sent Me, I also send you" (John 20:21). The Church should plan to neglect anything which interferes with going.

LAST HOUR LOGIC

When Scripture proclaims, "It is the last hour," it truly is. For the message of the Gospel, *it is always the last hour*. This unique, special doctrine of Scripture is called "Imminence."

Many ease back into thinking there's still four months to harvest (John 4:35). If you want to know how a single individual like Paul did so much, read his disclosure in Corinthians. He lived as if the end of all things was at hand, as if the final curtain were always imminent.

> But this I say, brethren, the time is short, so that from now on even those who have wives should be as though they had none, those who weep, as though they did not weep, those who rejoice as though they did not rejoice, those who buy as though they did not possess, and those who use this world, as not misusing it. For the form of this world is passing away. (1 Cor. 7:29-31)

The Gospel is eternal, but we haven't eternity to preach it. One would think we had that long when we view the often leisurely operations of the Church on the Gospel front. We have only as long as we live to reach those who live as long as we live. Today, over five billion souls are alive—alive in our present world, not in an indefinite future age which needs to be evangelized. *It is the last hour.*

RUN!

To make sure the Prodigal Son was welcomed home properly, the father RAN! Ran! I have wanted to run, too, since the Holy Spirit charged my soul with this realization—*"It is the last hour."* The world's airlines have found me to be a good customer. One of Paul's favorite Greek words was "spoude," meaning "to stretch out the neck as a man running to get to the finish line." It is translated, "study, be diligent, be earnest, hasten, be zealous, be forward."

> *The Gospel is eternal, but we haven't eternity to preach it . . . We have only as long as we live to reach those who live as long as we live.*

Many churches are very active, but active doing what? To fiddle about with secular issues is one way to look impressively busy and "relevant." But to bring the Gospel to a dying world is the true relevance.

Giving all our thoughts to our personal spirituality, when the fires of hell have broken out, is like members of the fire brigade having a shave before answering a fire call. We can spend years "standing for our principles," when we are only justifying our church quarrels and prejudices. The command to evangelize is all that matters, snatching men from the flames of an eternal hell.

That divine command was not given in a passing mood of the Lord. God Himself is driven by the peril in which human beings stand without Christ. Calvary was His imperative!

"And other sheep I have which are not of this fold; them also I must bring, and they will hear My voice;

and there will be one flock and one shepherd." (John 10:16)

Jesus told the disciples on the Emmaus road, "Ought not the Christ to have suffered" (Luke 24:26). The same Greek word, "dei," is used in both these sayings of Christ just above. The word does not mean that it was fitting or proper for Him to suffer, but that He *had* to do so—that it was in Him to do it. The God who went to the lengths of the Cross did not do so to give us a hobby or an interest for our leisure time. Our Lord did not die to provide a minor occupation for a few church folk. He commands us to preach the Gospel to every creature. This task needs us all.

We would deceive ourselves, and lose the true meaning of the Word of God, if we were to think that this "last hour" were not upon us. It is! It is no use saying, "God's last hour is a pretty long one, so why hurry?" We only have today. In the most intense meaning of the word, it *is* the last hour. John may have written it long centuries ago, but he was right. There was no hiccup in his inspiration.

- It is the last hour for somebody whose toenails already hang over the abyss of eternity.

- It is the last hour of opportunity in many a place.

- It is the last hour of possibility to obey the command of the Lord when He said: "Go ye into all the world . . ."

- It is the last hour before Jesus returns.

PAID BY THE HOUR

Years ago, in northern Germany, I had the privilege of leading an elderly lady to the Lord. For most of her life she had been a church organist, but yet had never known Jesus as her own Savior. When she heard the Gospel and opened her heart to the Lord, she was overwhelmed with the joy of the Holy Spirit.

Three days later I met her again, but this time she was completely broken. Puzzled, I asked her why this was. With tears in her eyes, she told me, "I am already 70 years of age and have only just received Jesus as my Savior. I may live perhaps another five or 10 years, but I have totally wasted 70."

Of course, this touched me deeply. Then I said, "Yes, but I know what is going to happen. One day we shall stand before the Judgment Seat of Christ. But He will not be as con-

When an old person gets saved, a soul gets saved. When a young person gets saved, both a soul and a lifetime are saved.

cerned about how long we cut the furrow of our life for Him, as how deep. Five or ten years, all out for Jesus, are much more than having been a lukewarm Christian for fifty years."

Do you remember the laborers of the parable of Jesus? (Matt. 20:1-16). By the clock, some had worked only a single hour, but the farmer generously rewarded them, paying them the same as those who had labored throughout the day. Why? Because they had worked as long as they had the chance to work. This is the principle of God.

If anybody is worried about not having been at Jesus' side in the harvest when they could have been, the answer is to leave that with the Lord of the Harvest. Don't waste time on tears. Give God, from this moment on, wholeheartedly what is His due! The Apostle Paul's advice is this in Philippians 3:13-14:

Brethren, I do not count myself to have apprehended; but one thing I do, forgetting those things which are behind and reaching forward to those things which are ahead, I press toward the goal for the prize of the upward call of God in Christ Jesus.

As long as you have breath within you, you are in time to be in on the last hour, the last day, the last month or the last year. You are not too late for that.

Young people have a slightly different status in the same last hour, however. When an old person gets saved, a soul gets saved. When a young person gets saved, both a soul *and* a lifetime are saved. The young person has an hour which could be a lifetime, and what a glorious hour that can be! An hour full of love, joy, peace, purpose and security, even if the last hour lasted an entire lifetime. The only way to live tomorrow is to live in faith and activity for Jesus today.

I once prayed for an old and dying man. Suddenly, a strange thought challenged me: "What would you pray if you were in his place?" A famous politician who expressed his last wish asked for, "one delicious pork pie!" It didn't take long before I knew the answer for myself. I would ask the Lord to give me the strength and help to conduct one more Gospel Crusade! I would like to hit the bull's-eye once more, to once more lead 100,000 souls to the foot of the Cross of Christ. There is nothing grander than that, nor is there a more glorious way to die, than fighting on that victorious battleground.

GLORIOUS CRESCENDO!

For Nineteenth Century Christian believers, the thought of the coming Twentieth Century filled their minds. For them, the coming of this century strongly suggested Christ's soon return. Those Christians prayed for new power to evangelize the whole world within the one hundred years before the year 2000. The goal of world evangelization was often on their minds, and the thought filled them with much longing. God heard their prayers and honored their hearts' desire.

Marine scientists tell us that ocean waves travel thousands of miles, even under the surface and across apparent calm stretches. Approaching land, they develop a majestic crescendo, hunch their mighty shoulders, and build up in rapid momentum and volume to burst finally and magnificently upon the shore.

A glorious swell of Holy Spirit power is gathering to a spontaneous crescendo today, world wide, as if hurrying to the shore. The lifting of the waves proves that the shore cannot be far. Jesus is coming soon! *It is the last hour!*

The latter day Pentecostal outpouring of the Spirit began in 1901 and the truth of the Baptism in the Holy Spirit was recovered with signs following. The mightiest revival of all time has swept onward ever since like a wave from heaven. It was the same tidal wave which had started in Jerusalem nineteen hundred years before. A divine deluge of power, "floods on the dry ground" (Isa. 44:3), had blessed the world for two or three hundred years. Then through unbelief and worldliness it seemed to ebb. The church even taught that such power was only for the apostles and the early disciples. As if only they needed it! The Holy Spirit became a mere Third Article of the creed, locked up and relegated to the past.

ANOINTED FOR THE LAST HOUR

With this wonderful outpouring of His Spirit, the Lord gave believers the power to do the job. The first tasks God's people did were to evangelize and to send out missionaries.

John wrote of the "last hour" in 1 John 2:18-27, (portions quoted below):

Little children, it is the last hour; and as you have heard that the Antichrist is coming, even now many antichrists have come, by which we know it is the last hour. . . But you have an anointing from the Holy One. . . . Who is a liar but he who denies that Jesus is the Christ? He is antichrist . . . But the anointing which you have received from Him [Christ] abides in you.

The Church is being anointed for the last hour. The spirit of the age would be antichrist or anti-anointed. The anointing

> *God Himself is driven by the peril in which human beings stand without Christ. Calvary was His imperative!*

of the Holy Spirit is a theme which threads its way through that first epistle of John. The apostle's warnings concerning the last times have come home to us today. They strike us with an almost frightening truth about our times. The spirit of anti-christ permeates human thinking and society. It is causing moral collapse. Hostile elements are raging worse and worse, like the early moments of a gathering storm. It is indeed the last hour.

God has His answer, however—the anointing for an anti-anointed latter day. He will never allow the devil to get the upper hand. The outpouring of the Spirit is His special provision for the last hour.

And it shall come to pass afterward that I will pour out My Spirit on all flesh; . . . before the coming of the great and awesome day of the LORD. (Joel 2:28,31)

Christ's whole Body on earth will be mobilized and armed for the last onslaught of the enemy. The devil will lose again. Satan is the eternal loser.

BIBLE PROPHECIES ARE HISTORY IN ADVANCE

This is the time of ripening for the final harvest. Both wheat and tares fill the field. Satan can see that his opportunities are slipping away—it is now or never for him. So the greatest display of wickedness, lawlessness and degradation is ahead. But believers have more to think about than mere survival. There are likely to be persecutions, and no doubt blood will flow. Our thoughts, however, are on triumph and conquest for Jesus. The build-up of enemy forces is being more than matched by an ever-increasing measure of the Holy Spirit.

When the enemy comes in like a flood, the Spirit of the
LORD will lift up a standard against him. (Isa. 59:19)

The greatest outpouring, the greatest anointing of God's
power ever known, is coming upon us. Past revivals will seem
as nothing when Pentecost breaks upon the entire Church. We
already get glimpses of it; the battle of the anointed against the
anti-anointed. We now know what it means in Revelation
12:11, "And they overcame him by the blood of the Lamb and
by the word of their testimony, and they did not love their
lives to the death." That showdown is fully described in
Revelation 12:9-10:

> So the great dragon was cast out, that serpent of old,
> called the Devil and Satan, who deceives the whole
> world; he was cast to the earth, and his angels were cast
> out with him. Then I heard a loud voice saying in
> heaven, "Now salvation, and strength, and the kingdom
> of our God, and the power of His Christ have come, for
> the accuser of our brethren, who accused them before
> our God day and night, has been cast down."

Bible prophecies like these are not alterable. They are
history written in advance! When the devil is out to trouble
the world, God will trouble the devil. God will do what He
said He would, even to the dot on the last "i." Hallelujah! We
rejoice! We know! The future is settled beforehand, and the
last hour is determined, with its very glorious conclusion. And
this is the period we are now entering!

In our great African Gospel crusades, there are mighty
victories over satanic powers and over sorcery. Gigantic piles
of witchcraft materials are brought and burned. Their owners
have been delivered from satanic fears and oppressions when
they received Jesus as their Lord and Savior. I often have
pointed to the flames, saying: "That is like where the final
home of the devil will be, in the Lake of Fire!" Satan is not
in control of hell's fire—those flames are his judgment. When

those "works of the devil" are reduced to ashes, we see the true Fire of the Lord fall on crowds "en masse."

The anti-anointing is a strange fire of destruction and death. But the flame from the presence of the Lord will devour it, just as it devoured the profane fire of Nadab and Abihu (Leviticus 10:1-2). After that, a sweet anointing of peace shall flow over the Church, all the way down to its feet and robe hems.

> *When the devil is out to trouble the world, God will trouble the devil. God will do what He said He would, even to the dot on the last "i."*

Let us forget old fights among God's people over issues which do not lead to the salvation of men and women. Our enemy is not another denomination or even denomination-alism. Our enemy is the devil, and the lies by which he deceives the world—the lie that God is dead, the lie that God is indifferent, the lie that we can do without Jesus. "They overcame him by the blood of the Lamb" (Rev. 12:11). Note that "him" is singular! We have one enemy—the devil. There is one power to oppose him—the anointing of the Holy Spirit: "and the yoke will be destroyed because of the anointing" (Isaiah 10:27).

Chapter 3

IMMORTAL WORK FOR MORTALS

A man with a mission needs vision. Isaiah and Jeremiah needed theirs. Without vision, they would never have moved forward boldly. To be called by God costs nothing, as God does the calling. To birth the call is another matter entirely. A man would soon give up unless he were called.

I was a hard-working missionary in Lesotho, but the dream of a Blood-washed Africa haunted me. The vision became more persistent and vivid. You must understand that divine pressure always accompanies vision. An all-consuming desire drove me to make my first ventures towards mass-evangelism. But I was still hesitant. The members of my mission board disapproved. They were good and spiritual men, but they lacked vision. Karl Barth noted that faith is never identical with piety. Normal missionary work was the fruitful approach to the salvation of Africa, they believed, not mass evangelism. Why did I think I could do it differently? If this was God's way, they asked, why were other men not doing it? While missionaries were content with the mission tradition—I was in turmoil. Were they wrong and was I right?

We have only one generation to save a generation. Every generation needs regeneration.

I felt isolated. Instead of lessening, the divine pressure on my spirit grew stronger. Then I met with a group of evangelists for fellowship, and everyone had a similar story to tell. They shared a common experience of official discouragement. They had the burning fire of the Spirit within, the challenge of vast possibilities around, but criticism from without. During these birth pangs, many times in agony of mind, I had to spend hours in prayer to keep my poise and peace. How long, I agonized, would it take to bring about a Blood-washed Africa without aggressive evangelistic crusades? We have only one generation to save a generation. Every generation needs regeneration.

The pressure reached a crisis point. One day I locked myself in a hotel room in Lesotho to pray. I was determined that I would not let go of God until I had a clear word from Him. I boldly put before the Lord exactly how I felt. I told Him that I was sick and tired of the strain, constrained to evangelize, but restrained by men. Was this really His will for me, this constant impulse to campaign? Other workers did not seem to believe mass evangelism was a good course of action. I was desperate for a clear answer.

That day God made matters absolutely clear to me. As frankly as I had spoken to the Lord, He spoke in reply. He said, "If you drop the vision which I have given you, I shall have to look for another man who will accept it and do what I want."

I repented of my hesitations immediately. I made my decision, forever. God then began to smile upon me and to send divine encouragement. Since that day, I have not looked back. I have learned how to handle critics and their criticisms by letting God Himself become my Defender. Let them see the Lord had led me by the fruit which it bore, I decided. Rather than concentrating on the critics, I have trained myself to concentrate on what He wants me to do. Since that time the ministry and the results have grown, step by step, dimension to dimension, sometimes rather dramatically.

"SKILLFULLY WROUGHT"

Evangelism happens to be my calling. There are other callings which will grip men and women—apostles, pastors, teachers, prophets, elders, musicians, organizers, intercessors, workers in a thousand different capacities. When God puts His Hand

upon us, He does two things. First, He gives us a ministry.
Then He opens a door to service. Each one of us has a unique
and vital place in His Kingdom. Every believer is individually
chiselled, "skillfully wrought in the lowest parts of the earth,"
as Psalm 139:15 puts it. Some are far from being run-of-the-
mill. They are hardly likely to be welcomed with a great
cheer.

A new vision can be disturbing,
not only to those who receive it, but
to those who don't, especially if it
puts a man in the limelight.   There
can be resentment, criticism, even
jealousy.   Sometimes a man's close
friends and colleagues can't believe
God has put a call into his soul. But
there is no accounting for God's
choice, as Paul points out about Jacob.
A call is entirely God's counsel, not
man's. If God calls, the best proof is
our patience when we are misjudged

> *We must be
> careful not to
> mishandle
> criticisms.
> Sometimes,
> through the
> eyes of others,
> you see the
> back of your
> own head.*

and criticized. The man who knows God has sent him will rest
in God, and leave those who disapprove or misunderstand for
the Lord to handle. "Therefore humble yourselves under the
mighty hand of God, that He may exalt you in due time" (1
Peter 5:6).

We must be careful not to mishandle criticisms. Sometimes, through the eyes of others, you see the back of your
own head. What others say about us is important, be they foe
or friend. I praise the Lord for those choice men and women
to whom He has guided me, for their perception and insight.
I would be a fool not to listen to them. Just like any other
minister, evangelists need advice. The evangelist cannot be a
law to himself. He is a member of the Body of Christ.

From my awful struggle and birth pangs in Lesotho, the Lord gave me the following insights and challenge to the Church:

A PARABLE FROM DEBORAH'S SONG

Isn't it marvelous how the Word of God lifts and stirs us? A passage in the Book of Judges unexpectedly gave me a mighty evangelistic challenge. In a unique way the Lord interpreted it in my thoughts, like a parable. In the period of the Judges, Israel had many ups and downs. Often the people were oppressed by invaders. In His mercy God would raise up charismatic leaders to unite them and to help them to defend themselves. One of these judges was Deborah, a prophetess. In her day a Canaanite king, Jabin, sent in his men under Sisera to plunder and kill.

Deborah was stirred to resist by the Spirit of God. However, she was no Joan of Arc, and did not deck herself in armor to fight like a man. She used her persuasive powers to inspire the men of Israel to rally their tribes under the leadership of Barak.

Each tribe received Deborah's call to unite and do what they could not do alone, to stand against Sisera. Some came, some refused. It is very interesting to see how the various tribes reacted. In fact, this old story is like a mirror held up to the face of the Church today.

DAN AND HIS SHIP SHOPS

Scrutinizing Israel after their victory, Deborah asked one penetrating question about the tribe of Dan—"And why did Dan remain on ships?" (Judges 5:17). The Danites were merchants, running a kind of mercantile marine service for Israel. They brought in goods from the far corners of the earth. Then, moored in a harbor, the ships became shops, selling directly from the importer to the public.

Now here is how I pictured it. Dan himself is at the till of his shop. The day has been great, the profits good. He is totalling receipts with satisfaction. Then, a sudden disturbance on the dock distracts him. A messenger, exhausted from the run, arrives with a dispatch for Dan:

"Dear Dan,

Jabin, the King of Canaan, has sent Sisera and is ravaging Israel. We are fighting with everything at our disposal, but we need help. The tribes must all unite to repel the enemy. Come and help—NOW. Your fellow Israelites are bleeding and dying. Please respond. Come at once!"

> *Greetings,*
> *DEBORAH*
> *(Judge of Israel)*

Dan, the businessman, was deeply moved. He jumped up and looked inland, where he thought hostilities might be in progress. He possibly heard the clash of arms and the crics of his dying brothers. But then, just as suddenly, he was moved by other thoughts. Awfully worrying questions troubled him. Could he just leave his money, uncounted? If he went and fought, what would happen to his ships and shops? Wouldn't he be risking his flourishing enterprise? And there was something else—Canaanites were his customers. He must not upset them. Shouldn't he remain neutral? What if his ships sank while he neglected them, enlisting in the army?

After such considerations, he decided. Hurriedly he stuffed a bundle of money into the messenger's pockets and said, "I certainly want to help. Regretfully, I can't come myself, but here's my contribution. Tell Deborah I'm with her in spirit."

Wonderful man, to let the women do the fighting! So Dan went on counting his cash while his brethren rallied round the standard of Deborah and Barak. Let others die for Israel, but

Dan had a business to attend to. There was Dan in his ship—the Ship of Self-Interest, Self-Love, and Greed.

Who does Dan represent today? It is for each one of us to ask ourselves. Dan is the Christian who belongs to the family of God, knows what the claims of God upon him are, hears the call of God, but does not respond to it. He remains in his ship shop when God wants him to "seek first the Kingdom of God." The music of the tinkling till, the applause of the unconverted or the opinion of family and friends deafen him to the call of the Living God.

> *Dan let Deborah down, but the undertaker was the last to let him down.*

In church Dan sings about "the sweet bye and bye on the golden shore," but will his ship reach it, or just flounder in the sea of life? If you think such situations could not be, just look around. See the wreckage of lives where people have chosen the wrong priorities. Some of the saddest people have been those with an eye to the main chance, who didn't keep their eyes on God. They lost their visions. Things went terribly wrong in the end. Success turned to ashes, popularity went sour. They chose the Danite opportunities of the ship shop. They let others follow Christ to His harvest field, or battlefield, or maybe mission field. And in the end they finally saw their joy and contentment turn to tragedy. "The harvest is past, the summer is ended, and we are not saved!" (Jer. 8:20).

MAKERS OF MONEY—OR HISTORY?

The runner with Deborah's letter hoped for a better response as he reached Zebulun and Naphtali. The two men were working in the fields and in the villages under the warm sun. The men were looking forward to the end of the day and to the joy of their wives and children. They huddled around the dispatch runner to hear and consider Deborah's call to service.

What should they do? Why, there was only one choice—
go! "Praise the Lord," they shouted, "that God has anointed
somebody to lead us. Now, let's make an end of this constant
harassment from Jabin and his bandits. Thank God for
Deborah! We'll back her to the hilt. Tell her we're on the
way. Count us in."

Zebulun and Naphtali exchanged their pruning hooks for
spears. Children were hugged, weeping wives kissed, and the
men marched away into the dust of battle. "Zebulun is a
people who jeopardized their lives to the point of death,
Naphtali also, on the heights of the battlefield" (Judges 5:18).

The war was soon won. But it brought no glory to Dan.
Deborah, a woman, had led Israel, and another woman, Jael,
wife of Heber, struck the famous final blow. She pinned
Sisera to the ground in her own tent with a peg through his
head, ending the rampage of his Canaanite army.

Deborah then traveled on her
judge's rounds and arrived at the
quayside to visit Dan. She wanted to
ask him one withering question—
"Why did Dan remain on ships?" Dan
sat still, his fingers fumbling nervous-
ly with a coin. He couldn't lift his
eyes to face this Holy Spirit-anointed
woman of God. Her question haunted
him the rest of his life. That question
will be heard again at the Throne of
God, when Dan and all the rest of us

*Zebulun and
Naphtali did not
have Dan's eye
for business.
Dan made
money, but
Zebulun and
Naphtali made
history that day.*

have to give account for our lives. Will Dan look at the Lord?
Or will he be too ashamed, not knowing what to answer,
hanging his head in confusion?

Zebulun and Naphtali did not have Dan's eye for business.
Dan made money, but Zebulun and Naphtali made history that
day, fighting and winning to save Israel in a remarkable battle
still talked about three thousand years later. They risked

everything, even life itself, fighting in the high places of the field. Dan staked nothing. He never took risks. When Dan died, he was the richest and yet most miserable man in the country, with bars of gold in his bedroom stacked to the ceiling, constantly within view so he could gloat. Dan had lived for gold for so long. Then, as his soul was leaving his body, Dan grabbed for his gold, wanting to take it with him. The angel of death swept him away with a laugh: "You've made your pile, now somebody else will spend it!"

The call of God is still heard by Zebulun and Naphtali people today, but not by the Dan people. Churches are composed of one or the other kind. The Dan people are those who consider their businesses more important than God's work, their back gardens more fruitful than the harvest fields, their homes more precious than heaven for the lost, and saving money more expedient than saving souls. "I have married a wife, and therefore cannot come," Jesus quoted a man saying who missed his opportunity in Luke 14:20. Zebulun left everything, though, and saved the kingdom.

Ask any pastor, and he will tell you who are the Dan or the Zebulun and Naphtali characters in his congregation. "It's always the same people who respond, and give, and work," pastors say. "If it weren't for them, this church would close." Some obey God's call at any cost, but others would not risk five cents for God. Zebulun and Naphtali died on the high places of the battle ground for God and for God's kingdom.

Jesus said, "He who loses his life for My sake will find it" (Matthew 10:39). And later, "Be faithful until death, and I will give you the crown of life" (Revelation 2:10). There's a nobility in that kind of dying, and even in one's readiness to give all, which we now recognize and honor on earth. But the Lord Himself will recognize it when a glittering crown of life is placed upon one's head by the hand of Christ Himself. Of the Dan folk, Jesus said, "He who finds his life will lose it," (Matthew 10:39).

THAT WOMAN!

After the battle came the celebration. Deborah the prophetess and Barak the general sang a victory song, naming the tribes one by one. The song is full of irony. After Dan, Zebulun and Naphtali, they named Reuben, about whom it is written forever, as if in stone: "The divisions of Reuben have great searchings of heart" (Judges 5:16).

Let me continue to draw my simple picture. The Reuben crowd were thoughtful types, people of consideration and judgment. They were the educated, the talkers. When the sweating and dusty dispatch runner fell panting into their midst choking, "Urgent! Urgent! A message from Judge Deborah," Reuben quickly took the letter. Immediately he called an emergency meeting of the Council of the Wise. Together, they gave Deborah's letter the serious attention they always directed to every issue. The council sat down and first read the minutes of the last meeting. The members pondered the situation. They were keen thinkers. Their perceptions soon showed them it was too big a matter for any rash decision, a decision which might later be regretted. With their usual caution, it was decided that they would sleep over the matter, and the council would meet again the following day with fresh minds.

There are others more concerned about spirituality and quality than about plucking men from eternal burning. They make fine speeches and adorn the platform in an elegant fashion, but they are absent on the front lines.

So, the next day, Deborah's call was carefully examined from every angle. The unanimous conclusion was recorded in the minutes—action was needed! But, a plan had to be devised before they could rush into battle. Another whole day was gladly devoted to these very important matters. The council would ensure the success of the battle. They would be a first-class army. The planning all took time, they reasoned, but it was better that they go well-prepared.

During that session, they had a coffee break and went out to stretch their legs, feeling very content with their work thus far. While strolling, the Reubenites caught a faint sound of the distant struggle and saw the smoke of burning villages in the sky. A straggler staggered into view, bleeding from his wounds. Thankfully, they felt they already were working on a project to help. Meanwhile, the battle raged on.

> *Evangelism, saving souls, is an emergency operation, and to a drowning man it would be quite irrelevant whether a man or a woman threw him the life-line.*

There was one last difficulty that still troubled them. The council met again the following day, and at last had to put the matter on the agenda. The problem was—Deborah! After all, she was a woman! How could they consider the call of a mere female? Where were the grounds for that in their Scriptures? When had a woman ever taken the lead—except to lead Adam into sin? Deborah stood between them and action. Their learning and knowledge saw no way to permit themselves to go at her call. The action had no precedent. A female taking authority to govern and to judge? Could God bless men following a woman into battle? It soon became clear: their duty was to decline to go. It was a matter of principle.

Is any of this sounding familiar? People today often don't like the way things are being done. They don't like the leadership, or the method, or the timing, or the personnel. Sometimes intellectual objections are found. "Evangelism—what with all our education? This is not the age of Paul and Peter! Soul saving? Revivalism? That was all fine for backwoodsmen, but we need a different approach." Yet, these people never find a different method.

Some have a Gospel of loaves and fishes. Jesus said, "Do not labor for the food which perishes, but for the food which endures to everlasting life, which the Son of Man will give you" (John 6:27).

There are others more concerned about spirituality and quality than about plucking men from eternal burning. They make fine speeches and adorn the platform in an elegant fashion, but they are absent on the front lines. Some are ultra-devout, deeply concerned with the work of the Spirit within themselves or in their churches. An evangelist would disturb and interrupt what God had been doing these past years. They can't support evangelists. They say evangelists garner attention and deeper developments are hindered. So, the pious words flow and no effort is made. Precious people continue to die in their sins, just the same. Evangelism, saving souls, is an emergency operation, and to a drowning man it would be quite irrelevant whether a man or a woman threw him the life-line.

> *Some have a Gospel of loaves and fishes. Jesus said, "Do not labor for the food which perishes, but for the food which endures to everlasting life, which the Son of Man will give you."*

ON VACATION

What was Asher's reaction? The dispatch reaches Asher in the hands of an anxious and exhausted envoy. His response? "Asher continued at the sea shore." Asher was on vacation. "I'm sorry," he told the collapsing messenger, "I need this rest. I couldn't break off my vacation, now, could I?"

Asher worked very hard in his job and had no time. Church duties were nice for those with nothing else to do, but he had his accounts to tally after business hours, and he owed himself this break without interruption. No, he couldn't come at the moment.

It is time to give consideration to things other than material comforts. Begin to labor for that which does not perish.

"But," Asher said, "I'm sure plenty of others will turn up and help. Some people are cut out for that sort of thing, you know. Deborah will be all right." Asher sat up in his deck chair and took a long sip on his cool drink. "Yes, tell her we admire her. She's marvelous, and we have confidence that we can leave the matter in her capable hands. God won't fail her. We'll be praying and believing for victory. Explain my predicament, that I need to stay here on the beach for a while, or I won't be any good to run my business."

Asher's philosophy? Depend on others to do what you won't do yourself. The sons of Asher say: "Somebody will turn up, and the job will get done. I like to spend my weekends where I can get away from it all. I have a place, and it would be silly not to go there." For some, anything they have planned, anything that crops up, any other demand but that of God has prior attention. They can't do all that *and* save souls. That is piling on the work. They need some relaxation at times, and some things have to be attended to. Commitments come first. They will help, sooner or later—when they are "free" and have nothing else to do and feel up to it.

Well, I visualized that Dan came to his tragic end. He let Deborah down, but the undertaker was the last to let him down. And Reuben, what happened to him? I hear that he dropped dead, still talking. As for Asher, he became overweight and had high blood pressure because of a lack of exercise. Asher never did a stroke, but had a stroke, and died. He lost his life saving it.

That is the parable from the story of Deborah. It remains a solemn matter for consideration in our own lives today. Jesus used humor when he spoke of a camel going through the eye of a needle, as he warned the rich about the difficulty they would have entering the Kingdom of God. People do make excuses, like the outrageous examples Christ used in the parable of the wedding feast. One declined the invitation because he had married a wife. Another had bought land, and yet another one had purchased oxen. They had their pleasures for a time, and then lost the crown forever.

Some in our own evangelistic team have already received that crown. A terrible accident occurred in 1985. We had been to Zaire, and a glorious Gospel victory had brought thousands into the Kingdom of God in the city of Lubumbashi. As many as 80,000 packed the stadium. Multitudes more were reached through live national radio and television broadcasts.

To die in the work of Christ may be the purpose of somebody's life. Christ is glorified whether people are won for Him by our deaths or by our lives. It is all the same.

After the crusade, our trucks were heading back to Zambia. Across the border, an unknown driver was drinking. He veered his tanker towards our convoy, colliding with one of our Gospel trucks. There was an explosion and two of our technicians, Horst Kosanke and Milton Kasselman, died in the blaze. The rest of the team stood by helplessly, praying and crying.

We were grief-stricken and shocked. Then, a spirit of determination triumphed. The work would not be stopped, not even by death and tragedy. "God buries His workers, but His work carries on."

However, some had another reaction. At home, the critics began to make negative judgments. "There must be sin in the team," they murmured. "Stop the work. Stop the ministry. Stop the whole operation." I was amazed. If there was sin in the camp, God would not need to kill two fine men to let me know! Those pointing fingers of accusation were like Job's comforters, who tried to prove his miseries were a judgment from God. These people were stay-at-home Danites, sitting in their rocking chairs behind their ship shop tills. They handed out advice without cost to themselves. And like the Reubenites, "they had great searchings of heart" from the confines of their comfortable armchairs.

To all such, we say that many are prepared to lay down their lives for Jesus in His work. Many a missionary has given his life for Africa. There are obvious dangers, such as the ones Horst and Milton met, but those brothers were prepared to risk all. Others will not risk five cents, let alone their lives. Our team members live with Jesus closely, day by day. We are on a real battlefield with Satan, who would like to destroy us. "The blood of the martyrs is the seed of the Church," wrote St. Tertullian eighteen hundred years ago, and his words have all history behind them as their proof today.

To die in the work of Christ may be the purpose of some-one's life. Christ is glorified whether people are won for Him by our deaths or by our lives. It is all the same. I offer this as my personal challenge to all who read this book—be a Zebulun or a Naphtali, and join the soldiers on the battlefield! The Lord is with us. Our Captain never lost a battle. It is time to give consideration to things other than material comforts. Begin to labor for that which does not perish.

To build God's eternal Kingdom means that mortal hands do something that will be immortal. That which is of faith in God can never die.

Levi left his tax collecting office at once, the fisherman of Bethesda immediately followed Jesus, and these people are living in our memories to this day. Now the call is to us. Jesus says, "Follow Me!"

Chapter 4

GASPING FOR THE GOSPEL!

If ten thousand people live around a church, according to statistics, four of them die every week. It is hardly satisfactory, then, if only one is saved every month, or even every week.

The need of the Gospel is absolutely critical, yet the devil devises tricks to hide the obvious.

Satan first tried to stop the birth of the Savior. He launched hell's missiles at all of Christ's human ancestors, finally slaughtering the innocents in Bethlehem. His policies of murder and genocide having failed, his only other alternative was to prevent the preaching of the Gospel.

At first, the devil used only persecution and false gospels, but over the centuries he has built up a considerable armory. One type of subtle weapon he deploys is to give believers other priorities. Satan doesn't mind how hard we work for our church, as long as it keeps us from spreading the mischief that the power of the Gospel brings on his evil kingdom.

Watch out! We can major in doctrine, in fellowship, in prosperity or in cultivating our own soul, in ways that bear no relation to preaching the Gospel to every creature. Let's not be fooled. We are in deception when good activities crowd out the most urgent work.

Did you know that the heart is so deceitful that we can even devise interpretations of the Scriptures that "let us off the hook" and quiet our consciences about saving the lost? Prayer itself, while so vital, must not be substituted for evangelism. But, prayer without evangelism is like an arrow shot into the air at no specific target. If we hold prayer rallies, they should be linked to some direct evangelistic effort.

The world's needs are vast enough for everyone to see, and it would take a book to describe them all. If anything can help the woes of the globe, the Gospel ranks at the top of the list. To preach the Gospel is to unbind, while to withhold the Gospel is to bind. Not to preach the Gospel means that we hide the medicine from the patient!

> *Not to preach the Gospel means that we hide the medicine from the patient!*

A lot of people have given up hope. They have seen the limits of science, technology, medicine, politics and education. Cynically, they turn to opiates to forget. Drugs, drink, anything—even religious mysticism. The idea that man has only man to help him is frightening. Evil grows two heads for every one that we cut off. This hydra-headed monster needs the dagger of the Cross of Christ plunged into its heart.

Every sphere of life cries out for the Gospel, like a fish gasping on the river bank for water. Personally, socially, globally, religiously, the *only* hope for us is in the Gospel.

THE GOSPEL IS THE ONLY NEW FORCE AVAILABLE

Isaiah observed that "The whole head is sick, and the whole heart faints" (Isa. 1:5). Sometimes our bodies cure themselves, but very often medicines are needed. These medicines reinforce the body's natural healing powers. Sickness can overcome the body's defenses, and sometimes outside help is then needed. When it comes to salvation, though, *there is no other source for man except the supernatural power of the Gospel.* Our task is to put that remedy on the table. There is no argument against the Gospel's wonderful power, just because there are some people who will not accept it. One can never force a cure on somebody, not even by threat, if the patient resolves not to take it. The person will just die, unless God in his mercy intervenes.

The history of Israel proves that when the Jews were true to their central faith, they did well.   But when they handed over their hearts to others, to new religions, heathens and perversions, disaster followed automatically.   The spiritual life of the people of Israel was always the deciding factor as to whether they prospered or were plundered.

To treat faith in God as a secondary matter, or as a controversial side issue, is fatal. We are what we believe. All activity is regulated by faith.

To treat faith in God as secondary matter, or as a controversial side issue, is fatal. We are what we believe. All activity is regulated by faith. If we don't realize that, then we do not know anything about human nature. God is the only issue that finally counts. It is impossible to exaggerate the urgency of the Gospel!

FIRE INSURANCE?

Now I want to tell you about the greatest need. One can't preach the Gospel as a mere social benefit. The Gospel has to do with God, and God has to do with eternity. If you want to consider the benefits here and now, they are obvious. To begin with, nothing adds up without God. Life is meaningless, as many atheists insist today. It is the typical cynical response of unbelievers who have no hope outside of Christ.

Most of us, however, realize that God confronts us with eternity. Our destiny is bound up in our response to the Gospel. "Are you saved or lost?"—that is the question above all questions.

The declaration of the Gospel is *"Jesus Saves."* He saves from wrath, judgment, hell, bondage, the devil and darkness. He saves us from dying in our sins.

Some jokingly scorn the Gospel as "fire insurance." But think about that for a moment. What is so foolish about fire insurance? It is a crazy householder who is not insured. People insure their houses and yet don't insure their eternal dwelling place. And we know that salvation is much more fabulous than a fire escape. Who else offers such insurance but Jesus?!

WHY HUMANITY SUFFERS

When I am interviewed by the press, one of the most frequent questions I am asked is why God allows so much suffering in the world. I have often pondered this question myself, not for the reasons that some jaded reporters ask it, but because I genuinely suffer when I see others suffering. So why does God allow suffering? You could just as well ask the U.S. Secretary of Transportation why he allows accidents on the highways. No doubt, he would take exception to your accusation and point to the rules of the road. "Every time a law is broken, an accident and suffering might occur," he would reply.

People suffer chiefly for one reason—they are ignoring God's rule book, the Bible, and everything goes wrong. Our Creator knows exactly how He has made us, and what will harm us. Consequently, out of a caring, protective heart, He says, "You shall not . . . " The "you shall nots" are not edicts designed to spoil our fun, but rather they are the manufacturer's handling instructions. God wisely knows that our psyche cannot handle sin and actually is crushed and tormented by misdeeds. It is always wise to read the instruction manual before using a new appliance. People take care not to break a tape recorder or a new washing machine but strangely, they don't seem to mind destroying their own spirits and souls with the poison of sin. Are you seeing more clearly that the need to preach the Gospel is desperate?

THE MEANING OF THE CROSS

Is the Gospel a call to discipleship? The question is debated. One matter is sure—Jesus asks no one to take up their cross until they have found salvation and strength at His Cross. We are not saved by denying ourselves and carrying our own cross. We are saved by the redeeming power of the atoning death of Jesus Christ, like the thief who turned to the Lord while dying on the cross next to Him. Of course, we hope many will become disciples and take up their cross, but first they must kneel at His Cross.

That Cross of Jesus consists of two beams, one vertical and one horizontal. Those crossed timbers are twin symbols of human misery and God's salvation. The horizontal beam is like a dash, the very sign used for a minus. And that is the human story. We were born with a minus, a deficit, a void. Sin has destroyed something. That something is missing, but people are at a complete loss to know what it is. They talk about their search for truth, but they don't even know what they mean by truth. They are like Pontius Pilate who, standing before Jesus, nearly fell over The Truth asking, "What is truth?" That is man's minus outlook.

Outside Jerusalem, a vertical timber was raised which crossed through our minus sign. Jesus hung there on that upright, and He thus turned our minus into a plus. The Romans thought the Cross was just an instrument of execution, but it was God's plus sign for minus-minded mankind.

But Jesus came, and outside Jerusalem, a vertical timber was raised which crossed through our minus sign. Jesus hung there on that upright, and He turned our minus into a plus. The Romans thought the Cross was just an instrument of execution, but it was God's plus sign for minus-minded mankind.

Jesus Christ turns loss into gain, lack into abundance, negatives into positives, night into light, hate into love, bondage into freedom, failure into success, sickness into health, weakness into strength, evil into righteousness and more—so much more. What a Gospel!

Indeed, give the Cross a second look, and it is even more than a plus—it is a multiplication sign. In John 10:10, Jesus declared, "I am come that they may have life, and that they may have it more abundantly." The Apostle Peter could write, "Grace to you and peace be multiplied." (1 Peter 1:2). Abundance is at the very heart of the Gospel.

That is why we must preach this glorious Gospel. Think of the many reversals the Savior causes. Jesus Christ turns loss into gain, lack into abundance, negatives into positives, night into light, hate into love, bondage into freedom, failure into success, sickness into health, weakness into strength, evil into righteousness and more—so much more. Praise be to God! What a Gospel! Nothing in all human knowledge can compete with that dazzling splendor. The greatest work on earth is to preach the Good News, and the greatest need in the world is the need for the Gospel.

In a British city where I preached, someone told me that contractors built a mosque and, as is customary, returned six months later to correct any fault which might have developed. One door was sticking, and they sent a workman to rectify the problem. But the Muslim leader refused the repair, explaining that if the door was like that, it was the will of Allah and must remain as it was.

Jesus leaves nothing sticking and wrong.   If it needs changing, He can change it, *and He will*.   His will is never faulty.   The purpose of the Gospel is to change a whole world which is wrong.   Hallelujah!

THE PRODIGAL PLANET

I cannot think of anything that makes more clear the urgent need for proclaiming the Gospel to every creature, than the subject of Eternal life after death.   True, other religions are out there.   But anyone who surveys them will know they are totally empty of any Gospel promise.   The mind cults of the East would offer only transient benefits, even if they did work. But the Gospel has more than mere mental poise in view.   The efforts the cults insist must be made to achieve harmony with nature are not worthwhile.

Jesus did not come to give us religious feelings or to suggest to us a system of mind power.   He came to *save us*, not to explain how our "inner resources" can be tapped to save ourselves.   Jesus was not a teacher of TM, or Quietism, or Stoicism.   He was and is, first and foremost, a Savior.

As for other religions, which of them offers eternal life *now*?   Some only promise the end of existence.   The teachings of "Karma" see life as such a misery that obliteration is the only way out!   Then there is the Paradise promise, which consists of endless sensual pleasure.   Unending gluttony and everlasting lust sound more like hell than heaven to me.

The supreme wonder of the Gospel is its present realization of *Life*—life of such quality that it cannot fade for eternity.

> Jesus said to her, "I am the resurrection and the life. He who believes in Me, though he may die, he shall live.   And whoever lives and believes in Me shall never die.   Do you believe this?" (John 11:25-26)

> *God loves His prodigal planet, and if we return, we shall enjoy the welcome of the Father and "begin to be merry."*

That is the highest Gospel possible! It is logically impossible to top it, and that life is available for us now. Urgent? The world is breathlessly gasping for the Gospel like a fish out of water. Eternal life is the most precious gift, and that is the number one message, as well as the number one reason, for preaching the Gospel.

This present world desperately needs the Gospel! Why did God make the world anyway? It was for good, for He is love. He filled it with the purest of pleasures that no man could exhaust, even if he lived forever. Every conceivable taste and delight, for every sense we possess, came from the loving heart of God for His children.

When we go God's way, it is all ours. When we resist Him, we resist His own concern for us. We spoil His plans to bless us, and happiness is destroyed. We have gotten to the stage today where we are brilliant at destruction, from the mess of graffiti upon walls to the threat of the obliteration of the entire environment. We war, we hate, we trample on the fair earth and foul all that He gives us.

Most of this destruction comes from sheer evil, or else from selfish greed. More basically, though, it comes from our turning away from God. Most of man's ills are man made. The Gospel reverses these fatal processes. It brings us back to do His will, and His will is always for the good of us all. God loves His prodigal planet, and if we return, we shall enjoy the welcome of the Father and "begin to be merry."

I HAVE SEEN IT HAPPEN!

God is mightily sweeping some parts of the world with the Gospel. The outcome is Salvation: sins forgiven, racial harmony, crime cured, stolen property returned by the truck load, marriages restored, families reunited, evil men turned to saints, death-dealing addictions cured and miraculous healings.

The Gospel is the most elevating force on earth. I have personally proven it. Many times during our Gospel campaigns in Africa, the police report that crime has dropped dramatically because people's lives are changed. I'll never forget how, in the nation of Burkina Faso, many big items—stolen refrigerators and other household furnishings—were actually brought to the preaching field by the repentant people who wanted to cleanse their homes from stolen property. The police had to come and haul all of it away in several trucks! And this glorious scene has been repeated in many other countries.

The Gospel was not given in order to level us all to the lowest common denominator, but to create new creatures, and give to all the dignity of the Sons of God!

The Gospel was not given in order to level us all to the lowest common denominator, but to create new creatures, and to give to all the dignity of the Sons of God! Men who once were savages are reclaimed and walk as princes. Hallelujah! What a reason to preach the Gospel! Could anything be more thrilling, adventurous and worthwhile? What else is worth life's effort?

The salvation of this world? Well, Jesus did not think it a waste of time to go out of His way to heal the sick and feed the feckless multitudes. He invited persecution for healing the man with a withered arm. From that moment on, He walked with a price on His head. But that man mattered to Jesus, and his arm had to be restored, no matter what (Matt. 12:10-13).

People who believe in the Gospel also believe in people and in caring for their physical needs. The less we believe in God, the less we value mankind. Atheism bred Adolf Hitler and Joseph Stalin, and put millions out of existence as if they were no more than figures in chalk on a child's blackboard! Preaching the Gospel is part of God's plan to put us, as it were, back in Eden.

> *Unbelievers will have to extract what drink they can from the dry ground of resentment, doubt and hatred. But the Spirit and the Bride say, "Come! . . . Whoever desires, let him take the water of life freely."*

But let's imagine the impossible—that science and politics could put us back in the Garden of Eden. Would that last long, and wouldn't our restlessness reduce it once again to ruin? There is one reason we desire Eden, and although many do not realize it—mankind wants those conditions again in which they heard the voice of God in the Garden. No mansion would suit a bride without her bridegroom! *No earthly paradise would suit us without the love and words of God.*

Some churchmen say that "man is a social animal," as if the herd instinct was all that could be mentioned about that marvelous creation called man. We are more than a herd—we are each made for God, and nothing else but a relationship with Him will ever satisfy us.

Sometimes, when inspired music touches us, we get a sense of infinity. Music only points to it, though. The music echoes a faraway greatness that it cannot fulfill. That infinity is God Himself, and what music only suggests is given to us when we receive salvation through Jesus Christ and begin to worship Him.

God is our natural habitat. In Him we move and have our being. Until we find Him, as we do when we obey the Gospel, we are caged. Men everywhere are beating their heads against the bars of their own materialism and unbelief. Their very money becomes their prison. Deep calls to deep, and height to height, within our souls. Our art, our poetry, our works of beauty are the expressions of imprisoned creatures who remember the glories of the free air and the mountains. While good in themselves, these expressions remain mere reflections of reality until a soul comes into salvation. Jesus is the reality behind all that we see or do. The Gospel releases us from bondage, allowing us to come into our true element!

Somebody said that "Christians are happy in their way." In their way? In what sort of way are unbelievers happy? In no sort of way, I think. Christians are happy in God's way, the originally intended way. The God scene is the only scene. Outside are the wastes of the wilderness and the horizons where dawn never breaks, where the godless will never be happy in any way. Unbelievers will have to extract what drink they can from the dry ground of resentment, doubt and hatred. But the Spirit and the Bride say, "Come! . . . Whoever desires, let him take the water of life freely" (Rev. 22:17). A way of life is preached in the Gospel that leads more and more unto the perfect day. That is another reason for the need to preach the Gospel.

COULD THERE BE A GREATER URGENCY?

Part II
The Incendiary Gospel

Chapter 5

GOD'S NEW ELISHAS

THE GREAT COMMISSION TO EACH GENERATION

Christ's "Great Commission" is not a scrap of paper, blown to our feet from centuries ago. It is Jesus, standing in the midst of His Church forever, saying, "Go . . . lo, I am with you."

Suppose Jesus said it to you personally—would you take more notice of it? Just imagine that you had a vision of the Lord in your church, like John experienced on Patmos. Suppose that Jesus spoke to everybody, saying, "Go into all the world and preach the Gospel to every creature . . . and these signs will follow those who believe" (Mark 16:15,17). What would you do? Would you continue living with a business as usual attitude? Or would you press on more urgently to witness for Christ?

> *Jesus has no further word for us until His standing orders are carried out.*

If anyone wonders whether the Great Commission is "relevant" today, they may as well ask if plowing and harvesting are relevant or if getting out of bed is! "Relevant" is not the word. The task is urgent. It is supposed to be our existence. A Christian is a witness. The name "Christian" developed because it easily identified believers—they were the people who always talked about Christ. The Christian's business is not busyness, but witness. Witnessing is the commerce of the people of the kingdom of God.

The written commands of Christ in Scripture are just as immediate as if He had spoken to us personally in a vision. The Great Commission is "our baby," and our work in this task is not optional. The Lord does not ask, "Would you mind helping Me? I would like to invite you." In John 15:16 He says:

> "You did not choose Me, but I chose you and appointed you that you should go and bear fruit, and that your fruit should remain."

Anointing of the Spirit only comes with obedience. The anointing and the Great Commission go together.

Jesus was not talking about the call to salvation, but rather of the call to service. We do not serve at our discretion. The Great Commission is like a draft call up, not a suggestion for our consideration. "Go into all the world and preach the Gospel to every creature." We are not to go for the sake of going, but for the sake of being sent by Jesus.

In fact, Christ's command is much more than that. Jesus turns us into witnesses. He changes our nature by His Spirit within us. He did not tell us, "Witness!" He said, "Be witnesses!" It was a creative word. God said, "Let there be light," and light broke in upon us. He chose us and then made us light bearers.

"For we are His workmanship, created in Christ Jesus for good works." These good works are to show "the exceeding riches of His grace" (Eph. 2:10,7). If we do not show the world the riches of His grace, it would be foreign to our new nature in Christ. What the Holy Spirit had planted within us is the Spirit of witness. But we can become slack and let the light within us die down through neglect. Fruitless branches are purged by God.

Now we have a wonderful guarantee: when we go as He commands, He goes with us. Evangelism and witness are the way to be sure He is with you! Suppose we do not comply— is He still with us? Well, one thing is sure. The anointing of the Spirit only comes with obedience. The anointing and the

Great Commission go together. This is what I want to inspire you to realize now.

TRANSFERRED MANDATE

There is a word from the Lord for us today. His voice came to me from a corner of the Bible not always noticed, where He is speaking to Elijah:

> Then the LORD said to him: "Go, return on your way to the Wilderness of Damascus; and when you arrive, anoint Hazael as king over Syria. Also you shall anoint Jehu the son of Nimshi as king over Israel. And Elisha the son of Shaphat of Abel Meholah you shall anoint as prophet in your place." (I Kings 19:15-16)

Three men had to be anointed—Hazael, Jehu and Elisha. That is straightforward, and not very remarkable. However, what actually happened is another matter. This great prophet Elijah failed to carry out two-thirds of God's command. He never anointed Hazael or Jehu. In fact, we don't read that he actually anointed Elisha, either, but Elijah did go and find him. When his mantle rested on Elisha, Elisha received a "double portion" of Elijah's spirit. That is, the same Spirit that had anointed Elijah then anointed Elisha to carry out the same commission. Later, it was Elisha who anointed Hazael and Jehu.

There are no hidden secrets for superior saints. His instructions simply say, "Go!"

So now we see a very important fact—Elijah's commission, with Elijah's power, transmitted itself to Elisha. A dual transfer took place from the prophet who was leaving to the prophet who was staying. Elisha received Elijah's enduement, but that anointing was to fulfill Elijah's task. God's commission and authority remained when Elijah left, falling upon Elisha. The mandate was transferable.

That is a divine principle. God's call and His power are transferable. The Great Commission, and the promises that went with it, made the disciples into what they eventually became. The same commission and the same promises were passed on to us, in order that we could do and be what the first disciples did and were. *We are the heirs of the apostles!*

But the commission of Christ to us is far more important than Elijah's commission, and the promised anointing is even greater. Read it again:

"Go therefore and make disciples of all the nations, baptizing them in the name of the Father and of the Son and of the Holy Spirit, teaching them to observe all things that I have commanded you; and lo, I am with you always, even to the end of the age." Amen. (Matt. 28:19-20)

Note that the commission includes "even to the end of the age." That entails now, tomorrow and beyond. This means that, if Jesus did appear and speak to us today, He would say the same thing. He has never changed.

People want to know what the Lord is saying to the Church. He, no doubt, has many things to say, just as He did in the "Letters of Jesus" in the Book of Revelation, chapters Two and Three. But if we are not busy doing what He already has told us to do, He will only have one thing to say—"get on with it!" So hear what the Spirit says to the churches: Why wait for another letter when you have not opened the first one yet?

Jesus has no further word for us until His standing orders are carried out. Many are waiting for God to speak, but only if He says what they want Him to say. They wait and wait for God to give them a new direction. But how do they know He has a new direction for them? Or that He has a great new revelation? Or that He will give them radical instructions? The word from God I have is that He wants the old direction;

a witnessing Church, with evangelism in and through the churches. Let me spell this out as clearly as I can: until this major command is put into effect, everything else is irrelevant!

We should have a humble attitude and indeed pray that the mantle of earlier men and women of God will rest upon us. There would be no Church but for the release of God's revival power through them. Many of them were true Elijahs. They took up the Great Commission and became God's brightest luminaries.

John had the most current word of the Lord when he said, "I write no new commandment to you, but an old command-ment which you have had from the beginning" (1 John 2:7).

Jesus doesn't keep on issuing fresh edicts, like some governments do today. What He once said, He has said once—once and for all. His Word is still His will!

Whatever "new thing" He says is in His Word already. There are no hidden secrets for superior saints. His command is simply, "Go!"

A motorist waiting at a traffic light was inattentive as the light changed from red to green. An irritable driver behind him jumped out of his vehicle and shouted, "That light says, 'go'! Are you waiting for the Secretary of Transportation's personal confirmation?"

We also have a green light from God. Let's go!

NO HAND-ME-DOWNS

God's people need to hear from him directly. Jesus said his sheep would know his voice. We do not read that Elijah ever instructed Elisha to anoint Hazael and Jehu. Although he inherited Elijah's commission, God must have told Elisha personally. This tells us that even though we are linked up with the generations of God's people before us, the Great Commission is transferred to us by the Lord Himself. Jesus

> *God always operates with originals. His mandate is direct, and not by tradition. We are not copies from copies, but originals from The Original, Jesus Christ.*

continues to point to the original Great Commission, but He gives us personal, specific guidance as to our part in this great plan. God always operates with originals. His mandate is direct, and not by tradition. We are not copies from copies, but originals from The Original, Jesus Christ.

"How shall they preach unless they are sent?" (Rom. 10:15). The Spirit directs us. The Holy Spirit is the Spirit of witness. Witness is His purpose. The Great Commission is linked to the Holy Spirit. When Christ baptizes us into the Spirit, He puts into our hands His instructions to take the Gospel to the whole world.

Everything comes from the Master Himself—not in a general way, but in an individual way. Jesus alone is the Baptizer, and we please Him when we engage in the work He sends us to do. Christ has reserved for Himself the task of baptizing us, as individuals, into the Holy Spirit. We don't go to men for their power. Everyone can get his own Holy Spirit baptism direct from the Lord. We are not called by the will of men, but rather by the will of God. Paul begins seven of his epistles with just that emphasis. Along with the call comes the power, the enablement.

I can lay my hands on men and women, praying that God will bless and use them (and I have literally done so to what by now must be scores of thousands of people). We may lay our hands on people to receive the baptism into the Holy Spirit, just as the Apostles did. But Jesus alone baptizes. Jesus said, "I . . . appointed you" (John 15:16).

If the anointing had to be transferred from hand to hand since the Day of Pentecost, or if it could only be passed on by the early Apostles, the Church long ago would have become one of history's lost causes. But we can have fresh oil from the Lord. The wise virgins did not and could not share their oil (Matt. 25:8-9). Each of us must have our own oil, direct from Jesus.

THE PACKAGE DEAL

The Great Commission to the disciples is transferred to each one of us today individually, and it comes with the individual anointing of the Holy Spirit. The command and the power are one package deal. Jesus told His disciples to tarry in Jerusalem until they were endued with power, so that then they would be witnesses in all the world. Separate the commission from the enabling, and you then have either power without purpose or purpose

Separate the commission from the enabling, and you then have either power without purpose or purpose without power.

without power. Power tools come with the job. Go with bare hands and you will make little progress.

ONE WITH THE APOSTLES

I have looked forward with great joy to writing the next passage. If you grasp this, you'll never be the same! I began by explaining what Elijah had placed upon Elisha. Did you realize that the Bible says the same endowment came upon John the Baptist? We read that he came in the Spirit and power of Elijah (Luke 1:17). What made Elijah a great prophet, and what made Elisha a great prophet, was what made John the Baptist a great prophet, too. Jesus called John, the greatest born of woman.

But that was not the last of the matter. The same Spirit who was upon Elijah made the Apostles what they were. Still, it didn't all end there. The Spirit rested upon the martyrs and the confessors too, as well as on those who followed. Has He now vanished? No—the thrilling truth is that the Spirit which made them one with Elijah makes us one with them all. *He is still here and we are included in His company.* The Spirit of Elijah and Elisha, of John, of the Apostles and of the early Church has never left. He has been among men ever since, generation after generation. And this same Spirit is now our inheritance. We were born to belong to His company.

We are in God's revival team, right alongside Whitfield and Wesley, Finney and Evans, Wigglesworth, Price and Jeffreys. We share the platform, hand in hand with all of God's anointed ones. We—yes, we—come in the Holy Spirit, the Spirit and the power of Elijah. What belonged to the great men of God in the past is ours, and what is ours was once theirs. The Holy Spirit is the Spirit of the prophets, poured out upon all flesh today.

These believers were all Elijahs, and we now are all their Elishas. What they did, we shall do. Jesus said, "Others have labored, and you have entered into their labors" (John 4:38). We identify with them all. They brought us the flame of Pentecost right from the Upper Room in Jerusalem, and now we carry it further. What inspired them inspires us—the same Gospel, the same Book, the same love, the same Christ and Cross of Calvary and the same Holy Spirit.

The men of the historic revivals have passed away. All have gone except for the chief figure, Jesus Christ. The One who met Saul on the Damascus Road and Peter in Galilee—He is here! He is with us! He is still baptizing into the Holy Spirit.

Often with the same anointing, the same persecutions will come. The Great Commission, the anointing and opposition go together. As always, the followers of Jesus will be defamed and mocked by the wise of this world. They will consider you, a believer, to be out of touch if you do not follow them in their unbelief and in the so-called science of Biblical rationalism.

These who accept this rationalism begin with a non-miraculous creed, and then take the scissors to Scripture to make it fit.

If we share Christ's work, we share in His suffering. But if we suffer we shall also reign with Him (2 Tim. 2:12). If we are derided for our faith in God, we shall reign by our faith in God. When people say the same things about you as they said about God's people in the past, rejoice that you are identified with them! Whoever treats you as New Testament people were treated proves that you belong to that glorious New Testament

> *What belonged to the great men of God in the past is ours, and what is ours was once theirs. The Holy Spirit is the Spirit of the prophets, poured out upon all flesh today.*

company. When you carry out the same Commission they did, with the same authority, you also will have the same enemies. Whenever the devil treats you as his foe, rejoice! He is paying you the greatest respect and best compliment possible. *He is ranking you with those he hated in the past, the beloved servants of the Most High God.*

DAVID LIVINGSTONE'S PROPHECY

In 1986 we had one of our great Gospel crusades in Blantyre, Malawi in East Africa. Blantyre is named after the town in Scotland where the great missionary David Livingstone was born. Livingstone had planted a Christian mission in the area and had founded a city that now has 300,000 inhabitants, making it the largest city in Malawi today.

Let me quote from his diary:

> *We are like voices crying in the wilderness; we prepare the way for a glorious future. Future missionaries will be rewarded with conversions for every sermon. We are their pioneers and helpers. Let them not forget the*

watchmen of the night—us, who worked when all was gloom, and no evidence of success in the way of conversion cheered our paths. They will doubtless have more light than we; but we can serve Our Master earnestly and proclaim the Gospel as they will do.

The Elijahs, the Pauls, the Justin Martyrs, and the Livingstones all relied on us for this future generation. They expected us to take advantage of all their labors. We cannot be proud, only privileged!

Livingstone died in 1873. So we were there more than one hundred years later. What about Livingstone's prophetic word? Was it merely wishful thinking? I rejoice to tell you what we saw. The seed sown so long ago now is blooming into harvest. For instance, we ourselves, saw 150,000 gathered in a single meeting. The people of Malawi heard about the same God as Livingstone's, the same Savior as Paul's, the same Gospel as Peter's. We were there sixteen days, and tens of thousands responded to Livingstone's message as we preached it for him and for Jesus. It reverberated throughout the whole country. The Holy Spirit spoke to my heart and said, "You are walking on the tears of former generations." Suddenly, I saw it all. We are linked up in God in a movement that consists of His earlier workers, too, and so we are one with them all. We belong to their team, to their mission. We are reaping with joy where they have sown in tears before us.

We did not have this harvest because we were superior to those precious men and women, but only because the harvest season had arrived. Both those who have sown and those who reap will receive the reward, according to the Word of the Lord of the Harvest, Jesus. He said:

"And he who reaps receives wages, and gathers fruit for eternal life, that both he who sows and he who reaps may rejoice together . . . I sent you to reap that for which you have not labored; others have labored, and you have entered into their labors." (John 4:36-38)

This is harvest time—believe it! The world's multitudes have multiplied. The opportunity is vast, exciting. And we, you, all of us, are the privileged ones chosen to do the reaping. Knowing that so much already was done, long before we ever arrived on the scene, should keep us humble in the times of success. We must not fail the sowers. We have been entrusted with a great trust. We owe it to them to put in the sickle, or, better still, to use a combine harvester!

The Elijahs, the Pauls, the Justin Martyrs, and the Livingstones—all relied on us for this future generation. They expected us to take advantage of all their labors. We cannot be proud, only privileged!

A REMARKABLE MEETING

In 1961, at just twenty one years of age, I completed my Bible college studies in the United Kingdom. I then could go home to northern Germany. The route took me via London. My train was not due to leave until evening, so I had time to do some sightseeing. I just walked as my feet took me, without a plan, and somehow wandered south of the River Thames into the pleasant avenues of Clapham.

Then, at a certain corner, behind a high wooden fence, I saw a name on a door plate, "George Jeffreys." I had just read a book by this evangelist, and could hardly imagine that I had chanced upon the very house where that same man might be. George Jeffreys came out of the Welsh revival and, with his brother Stephen and other members of the Jeffreys family, had introduced the Full Gospel message publicly to the people of Britain. His work shook cities, and tens of thousands of people had witnessed mighty miracles. Eagerly I ventured through the gate and up the path, ringing the doorbell. A lady appeared and I asked, "Is this the home of the old evangelist, George Jeffreys?" She affirmed it was so, to my great delight. I asked, hopefully, "Could I please see Mr. Jeffreys?" The reply was firm, "No, that is not possible."

But then that deep, musical Welsh voice that is said to have held thousands spellbound with its authority, spoke from inside, "Let him come in." Thrilled, I entered, and there he was. He was seventy-two, but looked to me like a man of ninety.

"What do you want?" were his words to me. I introduced myself, and then we talked about the work of God. Suddenly, the great man fell on his knees, pulling me down with him, and started to bless me. The power of the Holy Spirit entered that room. The anointing began to flow and, like Aaron's oil (Psalm 133:2), seemed to run over my head and "down on the edge of my garments," so to speak.

I left that house dazed. Fours week later, like Elijah, George Jeffreys had been translated to Glory. I had been led to see him just before he died. But I knew that I had picked up something from this former Holy Spirit-firebrand evangelist. The Lord, I am sure, had arranged that meeting. How else would it have been possible for me to stumble upon this one house in a city of ten million people, when George Jeffreys was not even on my mind? Whatever this experience did for me, one thing I can claim. Seeing this man of God made me understand that *we build on the people who went before us.* The city of God is built on the foundation of the Apostles.

We can liken it to a relay race. One man runs with a baton, another man grabs it and runs, and then another and another—they all share in the race and in the victory. If one drops the baton, or even runs a little badly, the efforts of all the rest are spoiled, and the whole team loses.

In the book of Hebrews, we read about the "cloud of witnesses" comprised of the saints. They stand looking over the battlements of glory, cheering us on. We are running for them. We must do a little more than they did, not a little less. It is the last lap before Jesus comes. We cannot rest on their laurels. The great finish line is in sight. Do you see, now, what the following Scripture means?

> *The original Gospel mandate is impossible without the original power. The perfect strategy of God is complete. He included you in it, and He included me in it.*

"And this Gospel of the kingdom will be preached in all the world as a witness to all the nations, and then the end will come." (Matt. 24:14)

What is the theme of the hour, or the slogan for today? Not our theme, mind you, but God's theme. It is "Evangelism By Fire" which is, in and of itself, an initiative for revival. It is evangelism by the gifts, the power and the manifestation of the Holy Spirit—Pentecost is revival!

Do you find it hard to win souls for Jesus, and so have stopped trying? Well, shouldn't that problem be first on your agenda? What is first on your church agenda, or on your conference agenda, on your personal agenda? Is it a resolution that nothing can be done because times are difficult? God has a way for you, by His Spirit.

Dr. David H. C. Read writes about a young minister in a tough area of New York, who poured out his woes about the difficulties to a local policeman. The officer tried to cheer him up, saying, "The fact is, Reverend, this is not the kind of district for a Christian church." These words woke him up. What else, he thought, is a Christian church supposed to be doing, if not operating where the need is greatest?

Doubters like to be clever. They analyze the situation and point out the impossibilities with impressive language. They "prove" that nothing can be done, using words like pluralism, hedonism, insularism and narcissism, trying to show, with high-sounding terms, that the situation is hopeless. You would think that God hasn't taken all of this into consideration.

The doubters are wrong. This is God's reaping time. Something can be done. God has prepared for everything—not by might, nor by power, but by His Spirit. This is what we are to rely upon, not television, radio, money or education, as necessary as these things may be, but on the miracle power of Jesus.

We have only one generation to reach this generation. The original Gospel mandate is impossible without the original power.

The perfect strategy of God is complete. He included you in it, and He included me in it. We are woven and enmeshed into His plans which cannot fail. *If we know that*, then no matter what, we will be able to do it!

Chapter 6

THE MATCHLESS MESSAGE

Don't argue—shine! You can't conquer darkness by arguing with it. Just switch the Light on. The Gospel is power, power for light. Preach it. Then you are plugged in, and the light comes on.

God's power lines draw current from Calvary, from the Resurrection and from the Throne: "The gospel of Christ, . . . it is the power of God," wrote the Apostle Paul in Romans 1:16. He knew. He proved it. The world in his day could not have been worse: cruel, corrupt and cynical. Yet the Gospel changed it. The Gospel can do it again.

HOW TO LET THE POWER GOSPEL LOOSE ON THE WORLD

One preacher told me he wanted a transformer to reduce the emotional appeal of the Gospel, to turn the message from high voltage to low voltage. But converting sinners requires full Gospel power. Preach to convict and convert. Your job is not to entertain, not to make people smile and go home feeling cozy. Salvation is not soothing syrup. Save souls, don't stroke them! Smiling happiness will follow.

We have an example of a master evangelist in Acts, chapter Eight. Philip the evangelist had a divine appointment on the road with an Ethiopian official. The Ethiopian was the queen's financial chief, a man of business, with no time for small talk. Philip didn't bother to ask what the man's needs were in order to start counseling him for hours. No, he didn't fall into that trap. Philip knew the man's need was plain and simple: The Ethiopian eunuch needed Christ. Salvation is everyone's need.

Philip got down to essentials.   He "preached Jesus to him" (Acts 8:35).

What did Jesus preach? Jesus talked about Himself. On the Emmaus road, walking with Cleopas and a friend, He explained to them, going throughout the Scriptures, the "things concerning Himself." All His teaching goes back to Himself.

Jesus is the Beginning and the End of every Gospel sermon, the Alpha and the Omega of all witness. We are not doctrine mongers. We are not religion pushers. We are not enthusiasts. We are witnesses to Christ. He is the be-all-and-the-end-all of the message.

What did Jesus preach? Jesus talked about Himself. On the Emmaus road, walking with Cleopas and a friend, He explained to them, going throughout the Scriptures, the "things concerning Himself" (Luke 24:27). All His teaching goes back to Himself.

Take one instance, for example. After He had left Nazareth and begun His wonderful ministry, the Gospel of Luke tells us that Jesus returned one day and went into the synagogue. For 20 years He had attended that very synagogue faithfully every week. The custom was to allow men who were known, to read the Scriptures, and perhaps comment on them afterward. Naturally, when Jesus was present at the synagogue again, He was invited to do this.

The Gospel message is found in the Old Testament—in fact, the Old Testament is full of the Gospel. Luke tells us that Jesus read from Isaiah 61:

"The Spirit of the LORD is upon Me, because He has anointed Me to preach the gospel to the poor; He has sent Me to heal the brokenhearted, to proclaim liberty to the captives and recovery of sight to the blind, to set at liberty those who are oppressed; to proclaim the acceptable year of the LORD." (Luke 4:18-19)

No doubt, many in the synagogue knew that passage by heart, for those words had been read for eight hundred years. The scroll of the Scriptures was handed back, the synagogue leader took it with great reverence, kissed it, and put it away, to be forgotten until the next week. But, suddenly, that scroll seemed to become a stick of dynamite. The Word on the lips of Jesus produced effects all right. It awakened the drowsy congregation. He showed them that the Word was about Himself. There are seven distinct statements in that verse and they all apply to Him, as well as to the present.

> *"Today," He dared to announce, "this Scripture is fulfilled in your hearing." Thus He declared Himself to be the Anointed One, the Christ, the One to perform all those promised exploits.*

"Today," He dared to announce, "this Scripture is fulfilled in your hearing" (Luke 4:21). Thus He declared Himself to be the Anointed One, the Christ, the One to perform all those promised exploits.

THE ACCEPTABLE YEAR

The first six statements can be summed up in the last one, "to proclaim the acceptable year of the LORD." That "acceptable year" is actually the Jubilee year. The word "Jubilee" is a Hebrew word. It is God's idea or thought. The Jubilee was instituted to give everybody a holiday for a year, to set free all bondservants and to cancel all debts.

Unfortunately, it appears that the Jubilee trumpet was never blown. The nation had never had a sabbatical year, and that was a failure which God held against them. The Lord would have been delighted with such gladness—God's style is to promote happiness. Even though the country did not celebrate the Jubilee year, *God meant to have it.* His Jubilee would be far greater than Moses', as we shall see. The Jubilee of Moses is described in Leviticus 25:8-17:

> "Then you shall cause the trumpet of the Jubilee to sound on the tenth day of the seventh month . . . and you shall consecrate the fiftieth year, and proclaim liberty throughout all the land to all its inhabitants. It shall be a Jubilee for you . . . You shall not oppress one another . . . for I am the LORD your God."

The synagogue congregation marveled at this new teaching. They could not imagine the Shepherd of Israel with foreign sheep and were lost in this unfamiliar landscape of Christ's prospects for the entire world.

Proclaim liberty! Do not preach for effects, for pulpit display, or to charm, excite, or scare folk. Do not preach to calm people down. You can preach for all kinds of effects, but Jesus simply announced liberty. He proclaimed, that day in the synagogue, that the Jubilee had begun. He showed them what a true Jubilee would be—deliverance! It would be a Jubilee, not merely for Israel, but for the whole world. A Jubilee for people like the foreigners He mentioned—Naaman, the Syrian leper, and the widow of Zarephath.

The synagogue congregation marveled at this new teaching. They could not imagine the Shepherd of Israel with foreign sheep and were lost in this unfamiliar landscape of Christ's prospects for the entire world. The world He loved was too big for them. Their fears were roused. Then, murderous passions were ignited, feelings that were never too far below the surface in those days. Jesus' sermon certainly produced a response—the members of the congregation attempted to throw Him over a precipice!

Yet, His message was wonderful—freedom, deliverance, healing and no debts! But whatever the reaction, Jesus preached His Gospel. So must we.

The world He loved was too big for them.

Debt in those days was tragic. Fathers and their families became slaves and could never get free. Only the Jubilee could release them. The debtors could go home. If anyone did not go home, it was his own fault. The law said, "Go!" Any slave, following the Jubilee, was a slave by his own choice.

Jesus Christ has proclaimed the Jubilee for the whole human race. All that Israel knew about Jubilees now became only a poor image of the real Jubilee of the kingdom of God. Lives set free, sins' debts wiped out, deliverance for body, spirit and soul. There are no sweating slaves in that Kingdom. No fetters. Nobody devil-driven. Hallelujah! What a Jubilee! Isaiah describes it:

> To give them beauty for ashes, the oil of joy for mourning, the garment of praise for the spirit of heaviness . . . They shall rebuild the old ruins, they shall raise up the former desolations, and they shall repair the ruined cities . . . eat the riches of the Gentiles, . . . Everlasting joy shall be theirs . . . no longer be termed Forsaken . . . Salvation is coming . . . and they shall call them The Holy People, the Redeemed of the LORD. (Isa.61:3,4,6,7; 62:4,11,12)

In Nazareth, the Lord turned these old Scriptures into a royal proclamation of a new dispensation. He announced an amnesty for all prisoners of the devil—"He led captivity captive" (Eph. 4:8).

"Sin shall not have dominion over you," explains Paul in Romans 6:14, because, "when the fullness of the time had come, God sent forth His Son, born of a woman, born under the law, to redeem those who were under the law, that we might receive the adoption as sons" (Gal. 4:4-5).

THE JUBILEE IS NOW

This is "the acceptable year of the Lord." High technology has not made deliverance unnecessary. In every nation, the enslaved abound—slaves to every contemptible habit, slaves to fear, slaves to doubt, slaves to depression. The devil never lets anyone out on parole. Everywhere people are failure-prone, sin-prone, morally defective, spiritually in chains. How ridiculous. Why? Because the Jubilee trumpet has sounded. People have been wonderfully set free—they just need to be told about it!

The Gospel . . . is a Proclamation of Deliverance. Dialogue? The Gospel is not open to modification. It is mandatory, a royal and divine edict.

So preach it! People have forgotten, forgotten that Christ has already come. This is not the pre-Christian era. We are not waiting for Christ to come and conquer. The war is over. Freedom is ours. Jesus has opened the kingdom of liberty and blown the trumpet of emancipation when He cried on the Cross, "It is finished!"

People who should know better are calling this the "post-Christian" era. As if the work of Christ was only for a past age! That certainly is not true. Christ opened prison doors forever, not just for a certain period in the past. The work of Jesus cannot be exhausted or undone. It's the greatest redemptive force at work on earth today. Never again can prison doors be bolted on human beings. When Jesus opens a door, no man can shut it. "If the Son makes you free, you shall be free indeed" (John 8:36). So why do millions needlessly languish in the devil's concentration camp? Today is the day of amnesty. The Conqueror has crashed through the gates, relief has arrived.

The most famous escape artist of all was Houdini, a show business notable. Police would lock him up in a cell and, as they walked away, he would follow them—already loose within seconds. Except once. Half an hour went by and Houdini still was fuming over the lock. Then a policeman came and simply pushed the door open. The door had never been locked! Houdini was fooled trying to unlock a door which had already been unlocked.

Christ has gone right through the castle of Giant Despair. He has the keys of death and hell, and He has opened the gates. So why are millions sweating, trying every trick to get out of their evil habits and bondages? They join new cults or old heathen religions, hear new theories, go to psychiatrists. But why? Jesus does set men free. He does it all the time.

That's the Gospel! You don't preach about it, or offer its contents for discussion. The Gospel is not a discussion point. It is a Proclamation of Deliverance. Dialogue? The Gospel is not open to modification. It is mandatory, a royal and divine edict. Some systems and theories of deliverance are bondages in themselves, full of life-long duties and demands. Only Jesus saves and calls us to Liberty.

I remember a man who told me that he also was a "spiritual counselor." However, he didn't believe that Jesus Christ is the Son of God, nor that the Bible is the Word of God. I wondered, therefore, how this "counselor" counseled anybody.

"Do they come to you and then go away with broken hearts?" I asked.

"Oh no," he assured me, "I just calm them down."

I looked him in the eye and said, "Mister, a man on a sinking ship needs more than a tranquilizer. Don't calm him down. He is going down already. When Jesus comes to a man in a shipwreck, He doesn't throw him a Valium pill and say, 'Perish in peace.' He reaches down His nail-scarred Hand, grips him, lifts him and says to him, 'Because I live, you will live also'" (John 14:19).

This is the Gospel of Jesus Christ that *must* be preached. Jesus *is* the Savior of our world. This message is life, peace and health for spirit, soul and body.

HOW THE ANOINTING BREAKS THE YOKE

Jesus said, "The Spirit of the LORD is upon Me because He has anointed Me." He is the "Anointed One" of this new dispensation. That is exactly how the first Gospel preacher, the Apostle Peter, understood it. He told his audience (the first Europeans to hear the Gospel), that: "God anointed Jesus of Nazareth with the Holy Spirit and with power, who went about doing good and healing all who were oppressed by the devil, for God was with Him" (Acts 10:38).

The expression "the Anointed" is the same as "Christ." To say, "Jesus Christ" is to say, "Jesus the Anointed One."

Now, was He anointed only while He was here on earth? If so, we should not call Him "Christ" any more. But if He is the same, then He is still the "Anointed One" today. That is what He is, exactly as is said of Him in Hebrews 13:8: "Jesus Christ is the same yesterday, today and forever." Not "Jesus" alone, but "Jesus Christ, the Anointed One."

This is also what we read in John 1:33: "Upon whom you see the Spirit descending, and remaining on Him, this is He who baptizes with the Holy Spirit." The Holy Spirit remains with Him, which is why He still baptizes in the Holy Spirit. This was an important point in Peter's first sermon in Acts 2:36: "God has made this Jesus, whom you crucified, both Lord and Christ." Peter's preaching was after Jesus' death and ascension. Following that instance in Acts, right throughout the New Testament to Revelation, Jesus is called "Christ" in every major book. Six times in the first ten verses of the first chapter of 1 Corinthians, the emphasis is on "the Lord Jesus Christ." And in chapter Two of the same epistle, Paul said: "For I determined not to know anything among you, except Jesus Christ and Him crucified" (v. 2). Just as He is still our Crucified Lord, He is still our Anointed One.

If Jesus no longer delivers, no longer heals, no longer saves, no longer casts out demons, no longer baptizes into the Spirit, then we have a Jesus who is no longer "Christ," for that is the very meaning of the title and name "Jesus Christ." He is "the same, yesterday, today and forever" (Heb. 13:8). If He has changed, then He has forgotten to tell us. But we have no evidence for any such thing! Hallelujah!

> *If He is the same, then He is still the "Anointed One" today. That is what He is, exactly as is said of Him . . . "Jesus Christ is the same yesterday, today and forever."*

Apart from the exact meaning of His title, what Jesus was *and is* also must be taken into proper account.

We will take up that issue in the next chapter.

Chapter 7

JESUS—ROBED OR STRIPPED?

When people go to church, they want Jesus. Not politics. Not sentimentalism. Not the man of Galilee as a distant, ideal figure. They don't want a phantom, a myth. If they have read the Bible, they want to meet that same Jesus in all His glorious vitality. Who wouldn't? Preach that Jesus, and the Holy Spirit is bound to reveal Him. He will step into the midst of the crowd, just as He promised.

In our crusades, both in Africa and elsewhere, we have seen the Anointed Jesus at work doing all He was anointed to do. We have seen Him sweeping into the world today with the winds of heaven. He has drawn together multitudes so great that they are only counted by the acre. Thousands are being saved, healed and baptized into the Holy Spirit at one time.

HOW TO KNOW WHICH CHRIST TO PREACH

When I see the miracles happening, miracles of healing, miracles of changed lives, miracles of cleansed sinners, I know Who is at work. It is the Anointed One. These wonders are His fingerprint, His hallmark. This Christ is the Christ to preach, the

Jesus can only be what you preach Him to be!

Yesterday-Today-Forever Christ. Every time we use His Name, *Jesus Christ*, it is a declaration that He is anointed to deliver. When there are wonders, that's how we know He is the real Christ. Miracles are His identity card, His genetic coding.

How did John know it was Jesus, in the partial darkness one misty morning? Jesus was on shore, way up the beach, while John sat in a boat 100 yards from the water's edge. Yet, he recognized Jesus (John 21:7). How? He recognized what Jesus *did*.

> *How many are guilty of stripping Our Precious Lord; men stripped Him once for His crucifixion. Unbelief strips Him again of His power.*

Jesus called to the disciples, telling them to cast out their nets, just as He had told them when He first met them. They had a heavy catch of great fish again, just as they had three years before. "It must be the same Jesus," John concluded, and he cried out, "It is the Lord!" Christ's actions revealed His Personage. But how can people know He is the same Jesus if He doesn't do the same things? How can they know Him if He is not even preached as the same One—the One who worked wonders and transformed human lives? How can anyone dare to call Him Christ and say that He doesn't work miracles? His anointing guaranteed that He would be a Miracle Worker. Jesus is *Christ Jesus*, the Anointed Jesus. He is the One to preach. Here is an important statement: *Jesus can only be what you preach Him to be!*

The Holy Spirit can only bless what you say about Jesus. The Spirit cannot bless what you don't say about Him. If "this same Jesus," the very "Jesus whom Paul preaches," is preached now, the Spirit of God will confirm it. Preach a limited Jesus, and He cannot be Himself. He doesn't save unless you preach a Savior. He doesn't heal unless you preach the Healer. How many are guilty of stripping Our Precious Lord; men stripped Him once for His crucifixion. Unbelief strips Him again of His power. He is no longer mighty to save and heal in many a church. As Paul expressed, He is "restricted" in our lives, which means "hemmed in with no room to work" (2 Cor. 6:12).

HOW TO MAKE THE GOSPEL NEWS

A schoolboy asked, "How can you call something news which is two thousand years old? Jesus is history, not news." The boy made a mistake. Only dead people are history. Jesus is alive and active throughout the world. He is a world figure, and all world figures are news, especially this One.

The word "gospel" comes from the Old English, "god" (good) and "spell" (message). It is a translation of "evangelion," the Greek original. The Gospel is not only what Jesus did, but what He does. Acts 1:1 states, "The former account I made . . . about all that Jesus began both to do and teach." He began to do it, and He is still doing it. He is making news today.

Two thousand years are nothing to Him. The sun is old, but active. The Bible is old, but powerful. If a telephone directory contains all the right numbers, I don't care how old it is, because every time I use a number I get through. I take the Bible, and every time I open it, I get through to the throne of God. The Gospel is the Word of God.

One of the greatest minds of modern times was that of Immanuel Kant, the German philosopher. He said, "The existence of the Bible is the greatest blessing which humanity ever experienced." It is, if it is preached. But it is a major occupation of some in the Church to spend time merely trying to find out who wrote it and when, as if it mattered. Meanwhile, millions die of spiritual hunger and are lost forever.

HOW TO MAKE THE GOSPEL HAPPEN

If the Gospel is just left as an idea—"the letter kills." But when it is preached under the power of the Holy Spirit it generates power. Under proper conditions, following the right formula, a process begins; something takes place. If you take the truth of Jesus and preach it with the power of the Spirit, you are using God's formula. Such a formula produces results.

When the Holy Spirit and Gospel preaching come together, there is an explosion of power. Divine energy is released. Paul used the word "energemata," which is "outworking energy." When such an explosion occurs, the Gospel is then news.

He came to set the captive free, not to renovate the prison cells or to make them more comfortable, with nice beds and color television. He wants people out.

When that heavenly force breaks upon us, with highly unorthodox and interesting effects. There is revival! The graveyard atmosphere is gone! Meetings cease to be mere form and ritual. This power is not a blind force. It is Jesus at work again!

The astounding fact about Christendom is that hundreds of millions struggle on as if Jesus were only mortal, not as Jesus The Christ. They talk about Him, but as the world's most conspicuous absentee. They act as if His first advent was entirely fruitless. They try to be brave on their own and manage, but haven't managed yet. It is mostly ignorance of the Gospel and its power, which can be blamed on us, the Church. Yet all around are Christ's footprints. There is the Church. Modern miracles. Bibles. Christian festivals. His sayings are part of our language. All that is best in civilization, our morals and principles, are here because He came. Yet people drag themselves through life as if they hadn't a clue. They creep in the shadows, afraid of the dawn. They talk of wanting a new religion, but have never tried the Christian faith. The trouble is, they have built their nuclear power plants higher than the churches. The nuclear age is powerless.

There is vast demand for the real thing, however. Too many suppose that Christianity doesn't work any more. The Church is a museum. The Bible may as well have been discovered in Tutankhamun's tomb—as if the Word were only for ancient Israel! That is why we must preach the Gospel in the power of the Spirit, with signs and wonders following. Then Jesus will step out of the Bible into modern life. Don't shut Him up in church. The Church shouldn't be His tomb. It often looks like it is, though. You would think some congregations were sitting around His coffin.

What people want from the pulpit is more than neat pulpit essays. We are not called to deliver sermons, but to deliver people. *People* are His concern. He came to set the captive free, not to renovate the prison cells or to make them more comfortable, with nice beds and color television. He wants people out. The Gospel is neither renovation, decoration nor reformation, but LIBERATION!

Praise God, it still works! Hundreds of millions all over the world are witnesses. They testify, "The Gospel has happened to me." News!

HOW TO HAVE THE ORIGINAL POWER

In earlier centuries in Europe, there was a most curious trade, the selling of relics. People hawked grisly skeletons and various other items which they claimed belonged to saints. Some of them were outrageous, such as one of Noah's teeth, or the iron filings from Peter's chains in prison. But behind it all was the pathetic longing to touch God's reality and power. They had no idea how to do so. They tried to do it second hand, through the bones and relics of apostles, martyrs and saints. They hoped these believers' blessings would brush off on them.

But why bother? The real thing is available first hand. Hallelujah! If we do what the Apostles did, we can get what the Apostles got. Peter himself said so (Acts 2:38-39). We all can know His power, and go forth permeated with Holy Spirit might. The original brand! For Paul it meant: "To make the

Gentiles obedient—in mighty signs and wonders, by the power
of the Spirit of God . . . I have fully preached the Gospel of
Christ" (Rom. 15:18-19).

Pentecost is for repetition in each life. The Apostles were
not extraordinary people, but ordinary people with an extraordinary God. "None of them shall teach his neighbor, and
none his brother, saying, 'know the LORD,' for all shall know
Me, from the least of them to the greatest of them" (Heb.
8:11).

HOW TO PLUNDER HELL
AND POPULATE HEAVEN

For over six years, I ran a Bible correspondence school. That
was in Lesotho, Africa, from 1968-1974. The purpose was, of
course, to reach the lost people of the country for Christ. The
enrollment grew to approximately 50,000 students.

To keep this project going put great demands on my faith.
I was only a missionary. I needed an office, and the monthly
rent was only thirty dollars. But one day I couldn't pay, and
I prayed and groaned all day, "Dear Lord, let me have thirty
dollars to pay the rent." The hours passed, evening came, but
I still had no money. Slowly, I walked down the road to the
house where we stayed as a family.

Suddenly, in the middle of that road, the power of the Lord
came upon me. I heard His Voice clearly inside my heart, "Do
you want Me to give you one million dollars?" One million
dollars! My heart raced. What I could do with that amount of
money! Why, with one million I could bombard the whole
world with the Gospel, I thought. But then, a different thought
struck me. I am not at all a weepy person, but tears began
running down my face, and I cried, "No, Lord, don't give me
one million dollars. I want more than that. Give me One
Million Souls! One million souls less in hell and one million
more in heaven—that shall be the purpose of my life."

Then the Holy Spirit quietly whispered into my very spirit words I had never heard before—"You will plunder hell and populate Heaven for Calvary's sake." That day, a determination gripped me. I knew God had greater plans for my life, and I set out to fulfill them in progressive stages. God has granted me ever-increasing blessing and grace.

How often since then have I seen the devastating power of the Gospel crash against the gates of hell, storming the dark domains of Satan! I often saw how, within one week, half a million precious people responded to the call of salvation in our Gospel crusades. I joked with my co-workers that, "If Jesus keeps on saving souls at this rate, one day the devil is going to sit alone in hell." I'm glad to make Satan sorry.

> *"You will plunder hell and populate Heaven for Calvary's sake."*

Knowing the power of the Gospel, we don't need to be frantic. Jesus is more than sufficient for every need. The world is sick, and Jesus has the only remedy—the Gospel. Our part is simply that we must carry this medicine to the patients. Jesus commanded it—*"Go!"* That is not a suggestion or a recommendation, but an order. We had better obey, or else miss the greatest joy known to man.

HOW TO HAVE AN EFFECTIVE GOSPEL

The message is Jesus. What He does shows who He is. The former is all-important. *Jesus saves from sin.* We are not moralizing. We are not giving descriptions of sin.

An American President went to church one day, and later his wife asked him what the preacher's sermon was about.

"It was about sin," he replied.

"And what did he say about sin?" his wife inquired.

We have a word from the King. The Gospel preacher is not an errand boy bringing a sealed letter, but one who has spoken to the King and understands the King's mind.

"Oh, he was against it," the President told her.

People expect that. The question is—what can be done about it? People need victory over sin in their personal lives. They need to feel clean, forgiven. Many a man will tell you that he knows he's not going to Heaven, but he has no idea what to do to resolve the dilemma.

We must major on how to get people out of the mire, how to be cleansed by the Precious Blood of Jesus, how to receive assurance and the witness of the Holy Spirit. These are mighty themes.

I constantly stand before vast crowds. To say anything less than the Gospel would be wicked. Thank God I have a Gospel, a positive message of power and hope. Then I find the fountain of the love of God springing up. Healing waters flow in all directions. His love touches human hearts. Men and women open up to God. They often have little of this world's good things, but it matters less when they possess the riches of God: assurance, peace and joy which no factory manufactures, no shop sells, no affluence provides.

We are Christ's ambassadors. The Gospel is a confrontation between God and sinners. Don't reduce it to a pleasant introduction. Our message carries the highest prestige. We have a word from the King. It has urgent priority. The Gospel preacher is not an errand boy bringing a sealed letter, but one who has spoken to the King and understands the King's mind. It is not a message for anybody who happens to be within earshot. The Gospel is not sent only to people who have a previous religious interest. It is for all, high and low, without favor. God is saying, "I speak," and sinners should reply, "I am listening."

The Gospel is not a proposition or suggestion. It is not thinking aloud, or an ongoing discussion. Preaching the Gospel does not mean setting forth the orthodox faith in a nice speech, like an actor's soliloquy to an empty stage. It is not an alternative, it is an ultimatum from the King—from God. "Believe or perish," because "God now commands all men everywhere to repent." That is what Paul asserted. His hearers were the lofty and proud Athenian intellectuals. But Paul showed them that God the Unknown was drawing near to them in love, stretching out His arms in welcome. The Holy Spirit takes the Word and points it as a sword, straight at every individual. Doctrinal study is not the same thing. The Gospel is God's "I," speaking to our "I," as a personal communication.

To preach a no-miracle Gospel results in the creation of miracle-free zones, which, regretfully, some churches are.

Next, we proclaim Jesus Christ the Healer. For us, our model is the Lord who proclaimed liberty and showed what that liberty was by healing the sick. The Gospel is not a defense of God. God defends us, hapless victims of the devil that we are without Him. Deliverance includes divine, miraculous healing. Some have thought healing was an incidental result, a mere attachment to the Gospel. Never! It is an ingredient of the message. We preach a whole Gospel for the whole man. Physical health is part of the whole package. It is God's special offer.

The Gospel is a miracle itself, and you cannot take the miraculous out of it. To preach a no-miracle Gospel results in the creation of miracle-free zones, which, regretfully, some churches are.

It is not addressed to guilty spirits, but to guilty men and women, suffering in their bodies for their sins. Jesus forgives and heals as part of the process. This is how it is preached:

"in demonstration of the Spirit and of power" (I Cor. 2:4). Otherwise, how can the Gospel be a demonstration of power if it is all spiritual and not physical? Christ is the Healer, and His healing extends in every direction—towards spirit, soul, body, mind and circumstances.

As long as the Church emphasizes the Baptism in the Spirit, the Holy Spirit will stimulate evangelism and missions. It is the same as a flower: Holy Spirit-evangelism carries in itself the seeds of its own perpetuity and increase.

Healing includes the authority to cast out demons. Demons sometimes may be directly behind sickness and depression. Not every sickness or weakness is demonic. Jesus made that distinction clear: "Heal the sick . . . cast out demons" (Matthew 10:8). The anointing of God rested upon Jesus to heal the sick, and the anointing of God rests upon His servants today for the same purpose, of course. It is wrong to underemphasize the healing of the sick, and it is wrong to overemphasize it. One can always fall from either side of a horse. Some evangelists only preach about physical healing. Certainly, wonderful things happen wherever there is faith, but people do not hear the message of salvation from sin. What use is it for people to be whole in body, only to be cast into hell? That is why, in our ministry, I do not speak of "healing crusades" but of "Gospel crusades." If we put all the weight on one side of the ship, it will keel over. To preach a non-healing Jesus is to present a non-Biblical Jesus, just as much as if we did not preach a saving Jesus.

The third ingredient is Jesus, the Baptizer into the Spirit. Jesus the Baptizer—but in fire, not in water. He is not just a "tongues" giver, or a spiritual gifts giver. He sends the Holy Spirit. In all our crusades, we pray for people to be baptized into the Spirit. I am not ashamed of this mighty blessing. I don't keep it dark "until people understand." It is part of the Gospel, and I am not ashamed of the Gospel of Christ. The Apostle Peter preached the whole Gospel in his first sermon, including the Gift of the Spirit, and so do I. The Day of Pentecost was not just evangelical. It was mightily charismatic as well! As long as the Church emphasizes the Baptism in the Spirit, the Holy Spirit will stimulate evangelism and missions. It the same as a flower: Holy Spirit-evangelism carries in itself the seeds of its own perpetuity and increase.

We must preach the Gospel in the power of the Spirit, with signs and wonders following. Then Jesus will step out of the Bible into modern life.

THE GRAND FINALE AND THE NEW BEGINNING

The statesmen and world leaders do not know what to do, despite all the knowledge and wisdom of this latter day. Believers know. The Full Gospel sees Jesus today, striding the continents to conquer. Hallelujah! He will ride on in majesty, the majesty with which He was crowned at Calvary, until He is King of Kings and Lord of Lords. He is now "absent in body" only. "This same Jesus" that we must preach will return. All little kings, lords and rulers will be pushed aside, and the world itself will be lighted with His excellent glory.

When believers come together now, they enjoy His Presence, but the world is insensitive and dead to it. Soon He will come, though, and all the world will know He is here again. He belongs here. He was born here, He lived here and He died here. He will come again to where He belongs, to His own. This time, they will receive Him.

This puts all His work together. We cannot leave it out of our message. For a warring, stricken, frightened world, this message is the only one to spell out H-O-P-E. Jesus is the

Hope of the world. We challenge the world. "Tell us," we ask, "how you think everything will be in peace? How do you think you will end up?" The world has no answer, no alternative. Let the world be ashamed, not us. Unbelievers have no hope. We have—Jesus. Preach Him! The world needs Him.

Chapter 8

WHEN THE MIRACLE STOPPED

APOSTOLIC TASK

If the Lord wanted apostles today, there would be no shortage of applicants. It is a noble title. But how many would want to be an apostle knowing what they really had to do?

I don't think it was to sit at the managing director's desk. Apostle means "sent one." What were they sent to do? First they were sent to be evangelists. Second, to suffer for doing it. Let me tell you—to witness and to evangelize is our privilege. We are doing what the Apostles did.

The Lord appointed the Twelve as His first witnesses. They were sent to introduce the Gospel to the world, and our task is to follow on. Their distinction as apostles was to initiate all evangelism. Jesus gave them His teaching, and they passed it to us. They were the foundation. We tread where they led.

"Apostle" was not a title of honor to make them famous. It described what they should *do*—(Go), and what they should *be*—(Prime targets for persecution, not for prestige). We read, "God has displayed us, the apostles, last, as men condemned to death" (1 Cor. 4:9).

The apostles were not divinely appointed church bosses. They left management to others. In Acts 15, the man who did that kind of thing, James, was not an apostle, because James the Apostle had been martyred already in Acts 12. We read nothing about apostles giving out orders. Their special honor was that "they were counted worthy to suffer shame for His name," and they rejoiced (Acts 5:41). Suffering as pioneers of Christ was the only high status they enjoyed.

In Mark's Gospel, the title of apostle was used because they had carried out a preaching and healing itinerary. Constantly, throughout the whole of the New Testament, apostleship meant one thing—preaching the Gospel. Paul said, "Christ . . . sent me to preach the Gospel." He began his great letter to the Romans with a clear statement of an apostle's work: "Paul, a bondservant of Jesus Christ, called to be an apostle, separated to the gospel of God" (Rom.1:1).

This was their area of authority. When Philip preached in Samaria and others evangelized in Antioch, the Apostles felt they had to give it their approval, as custodians of the truth, (Acts 8:14, 10:22).

Jesus had told them:

> "I will give you the keys of the kingdom of heaven: and whatever you bind on earth will be bound in heaven, and whatever you loose on earth will be loosed in heaven." (Matt. 16:19)

Peter is not jingling his bunch of keys at the gate of heaven, as some kind of celestial receptionist. That is nonsense. The figure of speech Jesus used simply meant that Peter was to be the first to preach the Gospel on the Day of Pentecost, thereby opening the Kingdom to those who believe. Peter's keys were the Gospel.

Indeed, the Lord made it quite clear that the keys were not exclusively in Peter's hands (Acts 1:8). The promise concerning binding and loosing was to all who believe and obey (Matt. 18:18). The loosing power is by the proclamation of the Word of God.

The apostles felt they were honored to carry out the task of evangelism. It was a sacred trust. They were responsible for a royal treasure. Paul wrote of it.

> "The glorious gospel of the blessed God which was committed to my trust. And I thank Christ Jesus our

Lord, who has enabled me, because He counted me faithful, putting me into the ministry." (1 Tim. 11-12)

He also declared that he was: "Paul . . . an apostle of Jesus Christ . . . [who] manifested His word through preaching, which was committed to me according to the commandment of God our Savior" (Titus 1:1-3).

So then, every apostle was an evangelist, first and foremost. But not every evangelist was an apostle. They are distinguished in Scripture each time the word "evangelist" is mentioned (Acts 21:8; Eph. 4:11; 2 Tim. 4:5). But evangelists share the chief privilege of the apostle in preaching. They do the apostle's major task. Evangelists are an extension of the apostolic arm.

They were not only "workers together" with one another but "workers together with Him." Partners with Jesus!

HE MADE ROOM FOR US

The apostles thought of their task as far more than just a particular job. It was the same work as the Lord Himself was doing. They were not only "workers together" with one another but "workers together *with Him*" (2 Cor 5:19; 6:1). Partners with Jesus! Part of the heavenly crusade team of the Father, the Son and the Spirit. The work of God Himself is world redemption, and the apostles were called to participate. So are we. God made room for ordinary men.

On their first mission, they jealously stopped anyone else from doing anything, but Jesus reproved them (Luke 9:49-50). Even later, they thought they had an apostolic monopoly on evangelism. But they had to recognize the ministries of Stephen, Paul and the rest. These evangelists were in true apostolic succession.

It is a strange apostleship which does not evangelize. It is a strange apostolic succession which does not carry out the specific apostolic task of preaching the Gospel.

I would like to relate how the Lord made room for me, also. Very many years ago I felt the Holy Spirit was urging me to visit a certain city. There were two churches there, so I wrote and asked for their cooperation. I received positive replies immediately. I did subsequently hear some negative rumors, but I left this with the Lord in prayer and remained confident that I should go. Nine months later, my wife and I arrived the day before the planned Gospel crusade. We met the ministers to discuss arrangements with them.

I can think of some things which would have been more useful than this discussion. We went around in circles, no matter how I attempted to guide the conversation into more profitable directions.

Discouraged and sad, my wife and I eventually went back to our hotel and had a little rest. I must have fallen asleep as soon as my head touched the pillow, for immediately God gave me a vivid dream. It was a parable. I saw myself with the same two ministers in a sports field, of all places, and doing the last thing that would have ever entered into my head to do—the long jump. One of these ministers tried first, ran and jumped, but did not do so well. The other followed and did much better.

It was then my turn. I began the run. As I ran, I felt something wonderful. An invisible Hand went underneath me and lifted me. I sailed gracefully over, airborne. My limbs were moving as if they were running, but my feet didn't touch the ground, and my speed was terrific. Then I touched the jump line and ju-u-u-mped. There I was, landing at the very end of the sandpit. Marvelous! An Olympic record! When I looked back, the other two men were far behind. In my dream, I threw my arms high with great excitement, shouting, "Oh my

God, You have made room for me!" I woke myself up shouting it.

This dream brought me great comfort by the Holy Spirit, and since that time, I have drawn encouragement from it. *God makes room for us!* When He sends us on His service, He opens doors for us. We can go! We may have to take a daring leap, as in my dream, *but we can take the long jump as the hand of God upholds us.* We shall land where He wants us. We will get there!

FILLING ALL EMPTY VESSELS

Churches may not always want to make room for evangelists. But I knew I must work with the churches. If I continued on independently, people might not see all that was involved. They possibly would think, "This is easy for him. He's not accountable to anybody who might approve or disapprove of what he does." So I wanted to get the cooperation of the churches.

That is one thing. There is something else, too, which I will explain. Here is a key Scripture. It is the familiar story of the never-failing cruse of oil (2 Kings 4:3-6). I would like to examine it. It will unlock some of the important principles of working with God:

> [Elisha] said, "Go, borrow vessels from everywhere, from all your neighbors—empty vessels; do not gather just a few" So she went, . . . and shut the door behind her and her sons, who brought the vessels to her; and she poured it out. Now it came to pass, when the vessels were full, that she said to her son, "Bring me another vessel." And he said to her, "There is not another vessel." So the oil ceased.

For many years my wife and I worked within the framework of a single denomination. God blessed us and used our evangelistic endeavors. Soon our Gospel crusades began to grow. Then, through this key Scripture, the Holy Spirit showed me what to do. I saw that the oil not only filled the woman's own dishes, pans, jars and bottles, but the neighbors' vessels as well!

The Lord said, "I do not have a burden for the empty vessels in your own house only (i.e., my denomination), but also for the empty vessels in your neighbors' houses. Go and collect them and fill their vessels, too."

"Oh," I replied, "my neighbors would never let me have their empty vessels. They would think that I wanted to steal them." (I knew pastors were nervous about other preachers drawing people after them—"sheep stealing"—they called it.) The Lord answered, "Build up an atmosphere of trust. Then they will lend you their vessels to fill."

That word of wisdom came to me in an early morning meeting with the Lord. It changed my whole perspective. In fact, it changed my life's direction. A new burden rested upon me for churches outside the denomination to which I belonged.

> *Every worker needs the Church like a fisherman needs a boat.*

Everyone must recognize the leadership of whatever body into which the Lord sets them, and that is Scriptural. "God sets the solitary in families . . . but the rebellious dwell in a dry land" (Psalm 68:6). A man should never become a law unto himself, whatever his stature, place or work. The eye cannot say to the hand, "I have no need of you" (I Cor. 12:21), much less can a hand tell the whole body it can manage on its own. Even the apostles did not have that attitude.

Every worker needs the Church like a fisherman needs a boat. The evangelist cannot sail away in waters of his own. God has set evangelists *in* the Church. An evangelist may find himself blessed and financially independent, but that does not mean he should sing a solo without the backup of the Church. He should not impatiently shrug every hand from his shoulder, no matter how he burns to win the world for God.

INSTRUCTED BY HEAVEN
TO BE INSTRUCTED ON EARTH

Take the case of that great servant Paul. As the persecutor Saul, he was making his way to Damascus, when a Voice spoke from the very Throne of God:

> Suddenly a light shone around him from heaven. Then he fell to the ground, and heard a voice saying to him, "Saul, Saul, why are you persecuting Me?" (Acts 9:3-4)

He recognized that this was a divine visitation. With his deep religious interests as a "Hebrew of the Hebrews" brought up at the feet of the great Rabbi Gamaliel, he must have wished a thousand times for such a direct contact with heaven. In his inquiring mind, so many questions simmered. And now, the moment of truth had come. What would he learn? What revelations of the will and purpose of God were about to be his?

Paul learned his first Christian truth, that believers are not a sackful of random elements, but a living body, the Church, and God did not allow him to bypass it. "Go into the city . . ." The Lord made sure of his earthly linkage.

In fact he was told nothing. Nothing except, "Arise, and go into the city, and you will be told what you must do" (v.6).

In the city! In Damascus were people he had come to haul off to prison for their "heresy" of faith in Jesus as the Christ. Now he was sent to them because he needed them, and was to become one of them. His first instruction would come from them, not by angels or voices from heaven. Paul learned his first Christian truth, that believers are not a sackful of random elements, but a living body, the Church, and God did not allow him to bypass it. "Go into the city . . ." The Lord made sure of his earthly linkage.

Paul went and submitted to the ministrations of others. We might learn from this man's wisdom and humility. A flash of light from heaven, an illumination of soul, a revelation of truth, and some men and women go off on an ego trip, independent of all counsel or oversight. They think they need not bother about those "in the city." But they should be wiser, for in the city, "there they will be told," and helped. Paul took the right direction from the beginning of his Christian life, and to him the Church of his fellow believers became strength and wisdom, as he to them. The result is history—glorious history!

In fact, we are all dependent upon one another, and if the evangelist needs the churches, the churches need the evangelist. The hand needs the body and the body needs the hand. We complement one another as do husband and wife. If churches ignore the evangelist, they shackle him. If the evangelist ignores the Church, he is like a life jacket with no lifeline attached.

So, having heard from the Lord and being guided by Him, I consulted my denominational leaders, and shared God's vision with them. God gave me favor. They were in gracious harmony with me, and with their blessing I was released for evangelism beyond their borders and across all denominational frontiers. From that time onward, I truly can testify that I have seen the oil of the Holy Spirit fill many vessels and very many churches, bringing multitudes of precious men and women to know Jesus. To God be the glory!

WHEN THE MIRACLE STOPPED

The widow's oil miracle eventually stopped. Why? Did God say, "That's enough for you today. I can't go on indefinitely"? He certainly did not. He still was pouring when they could find no more vessels. The widow said, "Quick, bring me some more bowls or jars from anywhere. There seems to be no end to this," but God outdid their capacity to receive. Then the miracle ended.

Some people are baptized in the Holy Spirit and they worry in case the experience will be temporary, the oil ceasing. The anointing abides forever.

There always will be oil. Zechariah saw a golden lamp which never went out, because oil for it flowed through pipes coming directly from the olive tree (Zech. 4). In the Holy Spirit, we have the source of all we need. As long as there are empty hearts, and as long as we go where God wishes and nothing restricts our movements, the oil will keep on flowing, always and forever.

Some people are baptized in the Holy Spirit and they worry in case the experience will be temporary, the oil ceasing. The anointing abides forever (1 John 2:27). But if we operate only with the vessels in our own little kitchen, the flow will soon cease.

It is no use praying for an outpouring of the Spirit week after week, just for our own small church, when the whole world lies outside waiting to be filled. "There is one who scatters, yet increases more," proclaims Proverbs 11:24. Every church should see its walls to be as wide as the globe, and its roof covering all people on earth. Call the world-wide revival your revival! The scope of the local church can be universal, when the assembly works alongside men whom God has given to the universal Church. Such a church will flow with Holy Spirit blessing.

If we shut ourselves in, and have nothing to do with those God has set in the Church, namely evangelists, we shall be out of the swim, out of the river of God. An assembly should not be a private club. In Germany, the beautiful, old Cologne Cathedral has a notice for tourists which reads: "This church is not a museum." What every church should be is a mission station.

TEASPOONERS

Others may have held back their larger vessels for fear of loss, like those when asked for a cup of sugar, give it carefully, a teaspoon at a time. Such selfishness stopped the miracle.

In my imagination, I think of the sons of the woman in Israel as they hurried down the streets asking everybody, "Have you a jar, or a dish, or anything we can borrow to put oil in, please?" Back and forth they went. Maybe some carping soul complained, "How many more things are you borrowing?" Others may have held back their larger vessels for fear of loss, like those when asked for a cup of sugar, give it carefully, a teaspoon at a time. Those who held back or refused to lend their vessels, helped stop the flow. Such selfishness stopped the miracle. We can help the miracle of revival blessing, or we can limit it to teaspoonfuls in our little kitchen.

It is necessary for all of us to work with others. Some may criticize, but we must not be put off. The widow's lads just smiled, knowing what their mother had in mind, and continued borrowing bowls for the oil.

God means to anoint us, not with a smear of oil, but with rivers of oil. When Jesus made wine at Cana, he didn't fill a few glasses, but made about twelve hundred pints, enough to keep them in wine for weeks—enough to get bathed in wine if they wished, so much that the bridal couple didn't know what to do with it all. Jesus fed the multitudes and had twelve baskets full of leftovers.

If an over-cautious church won't assist because evangelists could run off with their vessels, there will be no abundance for them. Ever since I have obeyed the voice of the Spirit, we have seen abundance. I, "being sent out by the Holy Spirit," began to work in harmony with the whole Body of Christ. It was like opening the sluice gates of a dam, and we have all shared in the flowing and endless waters of the river of God. Once we begin to calculate and protect our own little patch, the river is diverted. Insular people become isolated! Do we want floods of blessing? Then let the river overflow!

THE EVANGELIST'S INITIATIVE

Sometimes one has real enemies, raised up by Satan. It is demonic opposition. Then the anointing of God "breaks the yoke" and that anointing is the protection of God's servants. Often, carrying the battle right inside the gates of the enemy, I have realized that I am ringed about by the devil's forces, but those evil legions have been surrounded, also— by the angels of God! I know that, if the anointing were lifted, these forces would be upon me like a pack of

If churches ignore the evangelist, they shackle him. If the evangelist ignores the Church, he is like a life jacket with no lifeline attached.

wolves, ready to devour me in minutes. Enemies, critics, discouragers, they will come, but the anointed man or woman is undefeatable.

The devil is as a roaring lion, we read, which reminds me of the roaring lion that crouched to devour Samson. Samson met this young predator on his way to Timnath (Judges 14:5-6). The lion didn't know Samson, the anointed judge of Israel.

It had the surprise of its life—its last surprise, as it happened. A lion's snarl usually terrifies human beings, and they turn and run. Then they are easily pounced upon and caught. But when Samson heard the snarls, something happened about which the lion knew nothing: The Spirit of the Lord came mightily upon him.

When the Spirit of the Lord comes upon men, new things begin to happen. People begin to resist the devil, and he flees from them. Are you timid? By the Spirit, you shall be bold. We are like sheep among wolves, but the sheep are on the attack. We have power to tread upon scorpions, to walk the stormy waves. Experiencing the Spirit makes us more than a match for doubt and intellect. When we live in Him, we possess command, put demons to flight and bring deliverance for body, soul and spirit.

So Samson, the lion's intended victim, did not flee. Chasing fleeing victims gives lions an appetite for breakfast. But this man turned on the lion. The ferocious beast found itself facing a ferocious man. Snarling over his shoulder, the lion tried to slink off, but it was too late. Mighty hands lifted him. Later, his carcass became a beehive. Samson, with his bare hands, "tore the lion apart as one would have torn apart a young goat."

The Church was never constructed for defensive purposes. The gates of hell should be invaded. Offense is the best defense. Instead of waiting to ward off the devil's onslaught, turn the tide of battle and launch an invasion of the devil's territory!

Jesus came into the world, not to defend heaven, but as a conquering man of war to destroy the works of the devil. Christ took the battle into the enemies' camp, invaded hell, relentlessly flushed out the foe, hunted him down, drove Satan into a corner, gave him neither quarter nor mercy, bruised that serpent's head and left him defeated and useless. Satan is not "alive and well on planet earth." Jesus has mortally wounded him!

That is what evangelism does, in the Name of Jesus. Wherever the slimy trail of the serpent is, there the people of God should track the devil down with swords whetted. Give him no rest, for we are "more than conquerors through Him who loved us" (Rom. 8:37). The best way to defend the truth is to declare it without compromise. We have not been called to apologize for what God has said, but to proclaim it. "The sword of the Spirit . . . is the word of God" (Eph. 6:17). As David said of the sword with which he killed Goliath, "There is none like it" (1 Sam. 21:9). To defeat the devil, preach the Gospel. You'll never scare him off by shouting and noise. Use your sword.

THE EVANGELIST'S SINGLE-MINDEDNESS

Somebody asked an evangelist, "Why do you always preach on, 'You must be born again?'"

"Because," he explained, "you must be born again!"

The evangelist is a man with a driving urgency, not a man with two minds. The Gospel and nothing else on earth matters, neither fame, money, popularity or life itself.

No evangelist looks for a message to preach. "Woe is me if I do not preach the gospel!" He doesn't need to get together with other evangelists and say, "Let's discuss what we should preach," for all evangelists are totally without a doubt on that score. "Repent, and believe in the gospel!" (Mark 1:15). There is no point reconsidering it, since there is no possibility of a better message. The evangelist is a man with a driving urgency, not a man with two minds. The Gospel and nothing else on earth matters, neither fame, money, popularity nor life itself.

THE EVANGELIST'S AIM I

The evangelist is a gift *to* the Church (Eph. 4:11), *for* the world (Luke 24:47). The true evangelist is not interested in building his own empire. His aim is two-fold. First and foremost: *His work only makes sense in connection with the building of the local churches of Jesus Christ.* Everything he does should have this as its goal: that people should be brought within the Church, where the living Word of God is preached. The greatest, and even the most successful crusades, almost become meaningless when they are not conducted in the context of the Church and its growth.

Jesus told us the story of the good Samaritan, a lesson for evangelists. A man fell among robbers while on his way from Jerusalem to Jericho. The Samaritan found him and cared for him. Other men, priests and religious folk, passed by. After attending to his wounds, with oil and wine, and lifting him on to his own transport, a donkey, the Samaritan took him to an inn. There, in the inn, he was nursed and strengthened (Luke 10:33-35).

After we have begun to lift fallen people who have been wounded in life, we need to get others to help. The Samaritan found such help at an inn, where the victim was strengthened and nursed back to health. The evangelist finds it in the Church. There converts can be nurtured and built up in the faith. There they can become true disciples. Thank God for the inns along the road. Thank God for the evangelist who goes out to find the victims of the devil. The church/inn caring for the convalescent new convert will have little business without the Samaritan/evangelist.

It is like fishing. During our Gospel crusades, I always say that we, the evangelists, bring the nets and use the boats of the local churches. Together with them, we launch out and bring in a mighty catch of fish. Then we leave. We simply hand over the catch right there. We shake our nets out, repair and dry them, and go and lend a hand somewhere else. The evangelist gains nothing himself, except the joy and reward of seeing the Kingdom of God built up all around.

THE EVANGELIST'S AIM II

Secondly, *the evangelist's aim is to proclaim.* He proclaims the Gospel, whether the people will or will not hear. "And this gospel of the kingdom will be preached in all the world as a witness to all the nations; and then the end will come" (Matt. 24:14). A local pastor cannot function in this way. God obviously depends on other servants. But everybody should be heart and soul with the man who has the vision and duty to proclamation.

SPIRITUAL CHEMISTRY

To begin with, the Gospel is only news if it is preached. It is only power if it is preached, also. Preaching the Gospel is spiritual chemistry. Prayer brings power, but preaching releases it. Preaching the Gospel is like plugging into a power socket. The Gospel can't be used until it is spoken. Proclamation is absolutely part of the divine plan. People are saved no other way. This is the supernatural process. God instituted it for all mankind. "It pleased God through the foolishness of the message preached to save those who believe" (1 Cor. 1:21). It has pleased God that man should cast a net to draw fish from the sea, for fish normally won't jump ashore.

Jesus said, "Bring of the fish which ye have now caught" (John 21:10 KJV). First, catch them. Second, bring them. If churches never lift a finger except to let the evangelist preach, then do nothing to bring in what has been caught, the process the Lord intended has broken down, and the circuit is cut.

However, as Christ indicated, in some villages the Word will not be received, yet it still must be proclaimed (Matt. 10). This Jesus illustrated with the parable of the sower (Matt. 13:3-23). Not all sowings are equally successful, and some do not succeed at all. Why? There was nothing wrong with the seed

Jesus said, "Bring of the fish which ye have now caught." First, catch them. Second, bring them. If churches never lift a finger except to let the evangelist preach, then do nothing to bring in what has been caught, the process the Lord intended has broken down, and the circuit is cut.

(the Word) nor with the sower (Christ himself), but the trouble was with where the seed happened to fall. In some places, it produced nothing because of the ground. For the sower, the too-hard, infertile soil is frustrating. But don't be discouraged. Try somewhere else. Some preachers have no results because they preach discipleship to the lost and the need to get saved to the already converted. When a man works without results, he needs help, not criticism. Nothing succeeds like success in the worldly sense, and the successful in the Church get the praise. But we have a calling to fulfill, and success is not always the test of whether such a calling is properly done. "Preach the word! Be ready in season and out of season. Convince, rebuke, exhort, with all longsuffering and doctrine" (2 Tim. 4:2).

Failure is not the rule, however. The Lord sent us to the harvest field so as not to waste our valuable labors on a concrete strip or on a desert; He means us to bring in the sheaves (Matt. 10:14,15). Wait until the rains fall and the ground softens. Whatever comes, *we must* go into all the world and preach the gospel to every creature. Some will not hear, some will. When the Gospel is preached in all the world for a witness, then Jesus will come, He said. The Lord of the Harvest! So, to work, let us hasten His coming!

Part III

Personal Drive

Evangelist Reinhard Bonnke and his wife, Anni

The CfaN headquarters opens in Frankfurt, Germany, in August 1987.

The world's biggest Gospel tent, seating 34,000 people

The great Soweto crusade

On February 18, 1984, near the hub of Soweto, the city within the city of Johannesburg, South Africa, the Christ for all Nations Big Tent was dedicated to the glory of God.

Almost 200 000 people in a single meeting in Nairobi, Kenya, in June 1988

President Daniel arap T. Moi,
his Vice-President and eight government ministers
attend the Gospel meeting in Nairobi.

In Uhuru Park, as well as throughout the whole
country by television and radio, innumerable people
received Jesus Christ as their personal Saviour.

Reinhard Bonnke in the New Orleans Superdome

Evangelist Reinhard Bonnke was one of the main
speakers at the North American Congress
on the Holy Spirit and World Evangelization,
which took place in the great New Orleans
Superdome, July 22-26, 1987.

Signs and wonders were the order of the day
as some 40,000 people from 30 denominations
attended the event.

"But perhaps the greatest miracle was the catching of the new vision for worldwide evangelization . . . One of the most dramatic moments of the conference came as German-born evangelist Reinhard Bonnke finished a stirring though traditional salvation message. To virtually everyone's amazement, about one-third of those in the Superdome stood when he gave the altar call. To make certain that people understood what he said, he repeated his instructions — more people stood!" reported *Charisma* magazine.

Said Vinson Synan, chairman of the congress, "I have never seen anything to compare to it in all my years of ministry."

All 'heaven' broke loose
Record-breaking half million crowd in Kaduna, Nigeria, October 1990

Receiving the blessing of God

Largest evangelistic crusade in Islamic Indonesia — Jakarta, May 1991

Walking and leaping and praising God!

Tens of thousands are baptized in the Holy Spirit.

"Launch out into the deep and let down your nets for a catch." Luke 5:4, NKJV
Campaign in Mbuji-Mayi, Zaire, draws crowds of up to 360,000 in August 1991

JESUS CHRIST TE LIBERE

Great rejoicing
as witchcraft items are burned

The people of Freetown, Sierra Leone, receive God's miracle power with rejoicing at the CfaN Gospel crusade in December 1991.

Official state visit during the campaign

A campaign of "signs and wonders"
Both Christians and Muslims were hea

State President Joseph S. Momoh opens
the CfaN Gospel Campaign in Freetown,
Sierra Leone, December 1991.

A blind woman rejoices in her newfound si

And Jesus said, "Take up your bed, and go your way." (Mark 2:11, NKJV) Paralytic walks in Bujumbura, Burundi, August 1989.

Walking again after four years! Jos, Nigeria, November 1989

Jubilation as in Bible days during the Gospel crusade in Goma, Zaire, June 1990

◄ A mute boy speaks for the first time in Mbuji-Mayi, Zaire, August 1991.

After ten years of total blindness, he sees again in Bangui, Central African Republic, February 1992.

Photographs by: David Dobson, Gunther Hapke, Tom Henschke, Oliver Raper, Karl-Heinz Schablowski, Peter Vandenberg.

Chapter 9

THE SWIMMING LESSON FROM EZEKIEL

In 1991 a landslide for Jesus took place in Lome, the capital of the West African country of Togo. A whole mountain came loose in fact, and multitudes received Jesus Christ as their Savior. In this city of 435,000 there were as many as 200,000 people in a single meeting.

This is all very exciting, of course. But how can we see the whole world effectively evangelized like that? The Lord must have visualized it as being possible, because He commanded us to "make disciples of all the nations" (Matt. 28:19). Nations! I am sure that God has big plans for reaching mankind.

I go back again and again to the Word, trying to understand this thought, and ask the Lord to open my eyes.

I once came to a familiar Scripture passage, much preached on. The Spirit of the Lord was upon me and a truth in this passage exploded in my soul. It is in the book written by Ezekiel, one of the Old Testament prophets.

Ezekiel was a Jewish captive in Babylon more than five hundred years before Christ was born. The Lord often spoke to him through visions. These he recorded in his book, and here is one of them: "He took me into the land of Israel and set me on a very high mountain . . ." (Ezekiel 40:2). In the vision a man appeared to him whose appearance was "like the appearance of bronze. He had a line of flax and a measuring rod in his hand . . ." Ezekiel saw this man measuring out a new temple that would be on the mountain in Jerusalem, where the Jews would someday worship God.

After measuring the temple and instructing Ezekiel in its objects, laws and the actual sacrifices and worship that would be there, the man brought Ezekiel back to the door of the temple facing east; "and there was water, flowing from under the threshold of the temple toward the east" (Ezekiel 47:1). Ezekiel was led out of the north gate and around on the outside of the outer gateway which faced east toward the Jordan river. There Ezekiel could see the water running out on the right side of the temple.

Do me the favor of reading Ezekiel 47:3-7 with me:

And when the man went out to the east with the line in his hand, he measured one thousand cubits, and he brought me through the waters; the water came up to my ankles. Again he measured one thousand and brought me through the waters; the water came up to my knees. Again he measured one thousand and brought me through; the water came up to my waist. Again he measured one thousand, and it was a river that I could not cross; for the water was too deep, water in which one must swim, a river that could not be crossed. He said to me, "Son of man, have you seen this?" Then he brought me and returned me to the bank of the river. When I returned, there, along the bank of the river, were very many trees on one side and the other.

In the first part of this passage Ezekiel was taken from dry land into the waters of this glorious river. Many agree this is a picture of the life-giving flood of the Holy Spirit. What an experience! From the dryness and deadness of cold religion into the swirling reality of the Holy Spirit. What an excitement to come to know this side of Salvation! This thrill is unique and inexplicable—no wonder that the Charismatic/Pentecostal Movement continues to grow throughout the world.

In this remarkable vision, the Lord showed me embedded lessons that are essential for us to know if we do not wish to become spiritually stagnant.

ANKLE DEEP IS GOD'S MINIMUM

Four times, the angel carefully measured out one thousand cubits, leading the man of God in degrees. The first stage brought him into the waters that were "ankle deep."

Direct contact with the power of the Holy Spirit is absolutely wonderful, but do not forget that "ankle deep" is God's *minimum*! It is a tragedy that so many Christians seem to park in this position. It is sound advice never to follow a parked vehicle, because you will get nowhere. Don't follow a parked pastor or a parked church member, either. What I mean is, don't settle down to God's minimum. No doubt you can compare your experience with people who are not even ankle deep, but compare your position not with what is more shallow, but with the depth into which you can go. Many people have great potential in God but never get out of the baby's splash pool.

> *It is sound advice never to follow a parked vehicle, because you will get nowhere. Don't follow a parked pastor or a parked church member, either. Don't settle down to God's minimum.*

Once I was invited to speak in a prayer meeting to people who didn't believe in the Baptism into the Holy Spirit. I did my best, but it was very difficult. The people just sat there, wordlessly looking at me with big eyes. A little prayer was said, and it was all over. When I left the gathering, I concluded to myself, "It must be very difficult to swim in three inches of water." This, unfortunately, is the condition of many Christians. They paddle and work but make no progress, simply because they are grounded on the bottom. No wonder that things are so hard and wearing for them.

Charles Haddon Spurgeon wrote: "Some Christians sail their boat in such low spiritual waters that the keel scrapes on the gravel all the way to heaven, instead of being carried on a floodtide."

What an avoidable nightmare!

There are many frustrated workers. They are devoted, almost working their fingers to the bone. Yet so little happens. Why? Because they are only rowing at the brink. They are "do-it-yourself" people. They do the best they know how, and then "water it with prayer." They have not followed the Lord's instructions in Luke 5:4 to launch out into the deep. Today Jesus still stands on the shore and beckons us to launch out into the deep, to leave our shallow waters. But who will dare?

> *The success of the Christian is in the fullness of the Holy Spirit!*

What is the way of Pentecost? Jesus promised that we would do greater works because He would send the Holy Spirit (John 14:12-17). That means He would do the work. The Lord doesn't hand us a toothpaste tube from which we might squeeze a little drop of power once or twice a day, just enough for our spiritual survival. The normal Christian life is this—"He shall be like a tree planted by the *rivers* of water" (Psalm 1:3).

I say this with a shout—*The success of the Christian is in the fullness of the Holy Spirit!* Hallelujah! By the grace of God, I have been shown the secret: move into the deeper water of the Holy Spirit. Once in that flood-stream you will change immediately.

GOD'S PERSONAL APPROACH

As I visualized this scene with Ezekiel, I wondered why the man with the measuring rod took Ezekiel only one thousand cubits at a time, in four stages. When the Lord speaks, I'm the kind of man who likes to jump. So why not take the plunge at four thousand cubits all at once? The Holy Spirit taught me this spiritual swimming lesson.

The Father is very understanding of each of His children. He doesn't "throw us in at the deep end," altogether and all at once; spiritual growth and maturity takes time. His work is lovingly individual. The angel was instructed to first "measure" and then move. In the same way our blessed Lord measures our individual ability—and then leads us. If Ezekiel had been led four thousand cubits in one go, he might have drowned. But he made progress by going into the deep water in four stages.

The Lord brings us along gently. He wants us to go, but not to rush in brashly—that way we do not get cold feet or hot heads!

> *I am swimming in the Holy Spirit.*
> *His waters carry me.*
> *The Spirit lifts me.*
> *Swimming takes the weight off your feet.*
> *It gives your back a holiday and your joints go on vacation.*
> *He does the work.*

LEARNING TO SWIM

While I was thinking of this scripture one day God said to me, "Do you know what it means to swim?" Well, I thought I knew because I'm a good swimmer. But did I? The Holy Spirit caused me to see something I didn't appreciate before. He said, "When you are swimming you are in another element, and a new law operates. You have to let go and rest fully upon the waters of the river. Those waters carry you."

I see that now. I am swimming in the Holy Spirit. His waters carry me. The Spirit lifts me. Swimming takes the weight off your feet. It gives your back a holiday and your joints go on vacation. He does the work.

What, then, is the real handicap? The real handicap is to rely upon your own self, depending on your own energy and ability, and you will be trudging along the river bank, right beside the very waters which could bear you in their bosom.

Many are working for God, when God wants to work for them. He doesn't want us to work so hard that we drop dead for Him. I saw a gravestone once with a man's name and epitaph: "His life only consisted of work." I mused, "That is an epitaph for a mule, not a man."

God didn't intend for us to be beasts of burden, or to labor like robots. He could create pack horses in abundance, if that's what He wanted. But when the Lord thought of you and me, He had something in mind other than slaves. Our Father wanted sons and daughters with whom He could fellowship and feast at the table, sharing all He has with them. "All that I have is yours" (Luke 15:31).

It is time to change the negative image of the Christian life. Do you feel that becoming a Christian has simply bowed you down? That you never feel good enough? You feel like there's not enough prayer, or work, or love, or the Bible in your life. Duties overwhelm you. You could be in the glorious river of God being borne along by the Spirit. There are waters in which to float! In Him, you are more than a conqueror.

We are often like Joseph, who was taken out of a prison cell to rule. That is the principle of God's dealings all through Scripture. We are not to endure, but to enjoy our Christian life. I don't want to arrive in heaven to discover I had managed on five per cent of what God wanted me to have— that's no virtue. I am interested in the other ninety-five percent.

We need to understand the mind and the calling of God. As He led Ezekiel from minimum to maximum, so He will lead us, if we allow Him to do so.

A RIVER OF LIFE

The Bible doesn't have much to say about the sea. Paul was shipwrecked and Jonah ran to the sea to try to escape God's call, but generally speaking, it's not a nautical book. In Revelation 21:1 it states, "There was no more sea."

In Scripture, the sea is a picture to us of the masses of mankind and of the wicked and how they live. Isaiah wrote: "The wicked are like the troubled sea, when it cannot rest, whose waters cast up mire and dirt" (Isa. 57:20). Today we see our sea casting up on our beaches mire and dirt filled with the garbage of our lives. Contaminated hypodermic needles; soiled disposable baby diapers; discarded whiskey bottles; and the water filled with industrial chemicals strong enough to kill or cause mutations in the fish we eat. This same old water comes back day after day, the tide bringing the garbage we thought we had hidden away.

On the other hand, the Bible has a lot to say about rivers. Revelation 22:1 reveals "a pure river of water of life, clear as crystal, proceeding from the throne of God." Rivers flow— there's a constant freshness because it never has the same water.

A RIVER OF POWER

In his vision, Ezekiel swam in these deeper waters. All who discover this secret will have their lives and ministries transformed.

A few years ago, a completely frustrated minister of the Gospel came to visit me. He had just visited a psychiatrist and said that he no longer could carry the load of his church of fifty members. It was just too much.

"Are you baptized into the Holy Spirit?" I asked.

"No," he replied, "my denomination does not believe in it."

I took time to explain this wonderful truth and prayed with him afterwards. In the evening he left, but he didn't really drive home, he "swam" home! He had been gloriously baptized into the Holy Spirit.

What can God's maximum actually be? I certainly don't claim to have arrived at God's maximum. But I am definitely in transition! I am like the Apostle Paul, going from "faith to faith" and "from glory to glory" (Rom. 1:17; 2 Cor. 3:18). That is Holy-Spirit progression.

THE SURPRISE THAT FOLLOWED

God has something new every morning. After Ezekiel swam, he was returned to the river bank. This is, in New Testament terms, no anti-climax, because once we have been in the river, the river is *in* us. Those "rivers of living water" will be springing up within our hearts.

> *While God changed Ezekiel in His River, He was changing the whole landscape around Ezekiel at the same time. Conditions change with anointed people and anointed churches.*

This experience had transformed the prophet. Then, when he climbed the river bank, he looked in astonishment. "There, along the bank of the river, were very many trees on one side and the other" (Ezekiel 47:7).

Now He saw something that was not there when he had entered the river—T R E E S ! And this is the great truth of the chapter: while God changed Ezekiel in His River, He was changing the whole landscape around Ezekiel at the same time. Conditions change with anointed people and anointed churches.

I suppose if Ezekiel had physically been in Israel and tried to plant trees in that place, it would have failed dismally, even though he watered them with his tears. Yet God showed Ezekiel that He can do within seconds, what people haven't been able to do in many years. This is our faith for today! "'Not by might nor by power, but by My Spirit,' says the Lord of hosts" (Zech. 4:6).

People who flow in and with the Holy Spirit have reason to be astonished every day, because the Lord will be doing wonders. And, praise the Lord, nothing diminishes in God! Everything is getting more wonderful by the day.

DIVINE ENERGY

Another notable detail is this: those very trees already bore ripe fruit. While Ezekiel was discovering the depth of the River of the Holy Spirit, God had planted and grown the trees in no time. He is the creator of time and can shrink it whenever He wishes. "Their fruit will be for food," we read in verse 12. It was as if the fruit was beckoning him, calling, "Ezekiel, come over here. No more cooking using your own recipe. God has spread the table for you. No more disasters in your kitchen! A balanced diet awaits you!"

How wonderful! All of a sudden, the man of God was, and is, in partnership with the Holy Spirit. No more scheming until we are steaming. No more blundering in the dark. This is the wonder of a life and ministry in the Holy Spirit. This is how our world will be won for the Lord. Holy Spirit evangelism will win our generation for God! It all begins when we are obedient to the promptings of the Holy Spirit and follow Him out into the depths, where there are waters in which to swim.

IN OUR ELEMENT

Some Christians are always "in the wilderness." They sigh deeply and say, "I'm going through another wilderness experience."

The Christian who is not in the river of the Holy Spirit is out of his element. He's like the proverbial fish out of water.

We are not called to be desert dwellers, like the people of Israel were for forty years, even though the Lord had promised them a land of rivers. Christ has promised believers rivers, not as a rare exception, but as part of their natural environment.

We are not to be bank sitters, admirers of the passing waters, but river men instead.

Many times people have told me that, under their circumstances, they could not live a victorious Christian life. One young man in Africa explained that his grandparents and his parents were all witch doctors, and it was therefore impossible for him to live with Jesus in that place.

When we are in the Spirit we are unconquerable, invulnerable, going from victory to victory, our life hid with Christ in God.

However, not one of us could be victorious anywhere in this sinful world, if it were not for the Holy Spirit. Wherever we go, He is there. We move in Him and live in Him (Acts 17:28). He is our environment. We are baptized into Christ. We are swimming in the river of God, not in a little pool He created for us that is likely to dry up one day.

We may just as well ask the question, "Can a man live on the moon?" The answer is both "No" and "Yes." He cannot live on the moon if he goes there as he is. But, if he arrives on the moon wearing a proper space suit he can live there. The space suit contains the same air as that found on the earth. Wearing these space suits, the astronauts can walk, ride and jump upon the surface of the moon.

You cannot expect to live a successful Christian life if you are not in the Spirit, for that is how God arranged for you to live. Wherever we are, we can be in the Spirit, and that is the important fact. Even in the worst places, foul with the breath of hell, we ourselves are enveloped in God and can breathe the air of Heaven. "He who dwells in the secret place of the Most High shall abide under the shadow of the Almighty" (Ps. 91:1). He is our dwelling place, in every circumstance.

When we are in the Spirit we are unconquerable, invulnerable, going from victory to victory, our life hid with Christ in God. The man moving in the Spirit; the Church moving in the Spirit; workers, evangelists, pastors and teachers moving in the Spirit—that is the only formula I know for success. In the Spirit of God, we can win the world for Jesus.

Chapter 10

PASSION POWER

"The Love of Christ Compels Us"
(2 Corinthians 5:14)

LOVE LAWS

On the lips of Jesus, the law becomes love. There are Ten Commandments which God wrote on stone at Mount Horeb in Sinai. The first and all-encompassing commandment for Jesus is:

"You shall love the LORD your God . . . And the second is like it! You shall love your neighbor as yourself." (Matt. 22:37-39)

The voice of Sinai yearns. Israel misunderstood God from the start. Horeb thundered under the awesome weight of the Almighty. It was a powerful display, but it was the power of passion (Exodus 19:16-19).

LOVE RIGHTS

Who really was this God, whose words burned themselves into the very rocks?

He identifies Himself, and establishes His rights to give commandments. He has love rights:

"I am the LORD your God, who brought you out of the land of Egypt, out of the house of bondage." (Ex. 20:2)

That's who He is! His laws are love laws. The God who is a "consuming fire," is also a consuming fire of compassion (Deut. 4:24). He had come down to deliver an ungrateful rabble of slaves from servitude. He was set only on giving them nationhood and a new country. Such a task would make great demands on His inexhaustible patience.

THE IMAGE OF LOVE

God's own image in man was the image of love, until the storms of sin ruffled the waters and the reflection was distorted. But God was not outwitted. He invested all He had for every one who ever lived.

I've often wondered if when God made man, He might have shared His eager thoughts with the angels. If He had, would those spirits of wisdom have hesitated? "Such frail creatures of flesh?" angels might have speculated. "Will Lucifer deceive them? Will the devil and his hordes plot to destroy them?"

The God of all knowledge knew what would be. The first man ever born would murder his brother. But God had a master strategy. It would begin with Eve, and continue with all women. Their very instinct would be preprogrammed. Within their nature would be planted a mother's heart, the purest form affection can take, an affection which never seeks reward. It would filter through to the family and set protective standards. Then the great secret plan of God would slowly begin to unfold, through all the ways and woes of Israel. It would be unveiled at last, in the Son of His bosom.

"For God so loved the world that He gave His only begotten Son." (John 3:16)

God's own image in man was the image of love, until the storms of sin ruffled the waters and the reflection was distorted. But God was not outwitted. He invested all He had for everyone who ever lived. The Gospel blessed the ears of men; the Gospel was His heart, a revelation of troubled anxiety for His creatures.

FOR US AND TO US

Evangelism is summed up in this: *God loving us through His Gospel.* Every message preached should be winged with love. We are people loving people by God's imparted love. Through the ages, impassioned men and women have lived and died to preach Christ and His salvation to all tribes and nations. From the same divine force, the finest works of men have come: churches, charities, hospitals, orphanages, civilization itself. The love of God in a man's soul is one hundred times finer and more noble than any motive that has ever driven him.

> *The love of God in a man's soul is one hundred times finer and more noble than any motive that has ever driven him.*

When the Presence of God departed from Mt. Horeb in Sinai, what was left? The first answer is found in Exodus 21:5-6, another love law concerning bondslaves. A slave had absolutely no status, no rights, but a bondservant had the right to leave his master after his period of servitude was finished. However, if a bondservant married a wife, he could not legally take her away with him after he had served his contract with his master. He could keep his wife only if he stayed with his master in permanent servitude.

Furthermore, the bondservant who elected to stay with his master had to submit to a painful procedure as an outward sign of his submission. The ceremony was this: he would be taken to the front door of his master's house, whereupon his earlobe would be spiked through to the doorway. The nail would be immediately withdrawn, but the resulting scar would be an outward symbol that the man had chosen to stay with his master.

The scar would also be there, both in the ear and in the door, as if to say, "I love my wife and have given myself *for* her so I can give myself *to* her."

GOD'S EPIC OF LOVE

The bondservant is a parable of the love affair God has with mankind. Jesus was also spiked through—in his hands and his feet—in order to redeem his Bride, his Body—you and me (1 Cor. 12:27; Eph. 5:25-27). The great King of the universe humbled Himself to become a bondservant for our sakes. Christ gave Himself *for* us so that He could give Himself *to* us. God is love. That is what everything is about. That is why we were born, to love and be loved. To know the love of all loves is the secret of all secrets. Know that, and you possess the answer to the meaning of life. A loveless Gospel is a contradiction—a sea without water, sun without light, honey without sweetness, bread without substance. The Gospel is ultimately nothing other than the expression of God's infinite love for us.

From Genesis to Revelation, the love epic moves from eternity to eternity: "I have loved you with an everlasting love," God says to us (Jer. 31:3). Hosea heard the cry of God. Israel was finally wandering into the darkness of their long historical night, and Hosea was permitted to catch the echo of the divine anguish. "How can I give you up, Ephraim? How can I hand you over, Israel? . . . My heart churns within Me; my sympathy is stirred" (Hos. 11:8).

Jesus said He only did what He saw the Father doing. The only explanation given us when Jesus healed the sick, or did anything whatsoever, is always the same—He had compassion. Love Incarnate. In fact, the law of the universe is love.

NIAGARA OF LOVE

I don't suppose any angel ever asked the Lord why He proposed to create beings such as we are, with our freedom to choose evil and with our power to break His heart. The angels long to look into such matters. Whatever the pain, Christ had to pour Himself out in a Niagara of love. And what better than to pour it out on those who could never deserve it? What could better serve His purposes than enemies, the wicked, the oppressors and the oppressed seeking revenge?   These are those He would make "accepted in the Beloved" (Eph.1:6).

Hell is an awful and mysterious place. It is not a subject given us to enjoy. We are not meant to dangle men over the pit to see them squirm, simply because they are enemies of righteousness. Why, then are we even told of this possible destiny of sinners? We are informed about Hell in order to arouse our deepest pity and especially to drive us to care about and warn the heedless.

THE LOVE EXPRESSION ON HIS FACE

Jesus said more about hell than any-body in the Bible, and, in fact, almost everything said about hell in Scripture is something He said. I wish I could have heard how He talked about hell. In what manner did He say, "Woe to you, . . ." even to the Pharisees? What was His tone of voice, the look

> *He gave a new definition to the word love by going to the cross.*

in His eyes, His gesture of agony for His creatures? Certainly, no actor could imitate it, for His warnings sprang from a divine heart too deep to fathom. Only His love in our hearts could possibly give our voices the deep compassion of His warnings.

LOVE MOTIVE

Love was the motive of the Son of God who came among us. Look at these familiar words from Scripture: "Who for the joy that was set before Him endured the cross, despising the shame" (Heb. 12:2). Those who know best tell us that the word "for" in "for the joy," is a preposition better rendered "instead of." It doesn't mean "to seek joy," but "to sacrifice joy." After the Cross, He only regained what was His already. He, the thrice-blessed God, had exchanged His crown for a cross.

> *A loveless Gospel is a contradiction— a sea without water, sun without light, honey without sweetness, bread without substance. The Gospel is ultimately nothing other than the expression of God's infinite love for us.*

Again we read in John 13:1 that the time came for Jesus "to depart from this world." But He didn't go. Instead, He took a towel and washed the feet of His disciples, and allowed Judas to go out and betray Him. He went all the way to Calvary, and became a ransom for all the devil's captives. Then, in the same verse, John explained why: "having loved His own who were in the world, He loved them to the end." Jesus didn't go back to the Father with unfinished work. He gave a new definition to the word love by going to the cross. Before the cross, love had no adequate yardstick. After the cross, the cross itself became the ultimate way by which love can be measured.

ILLUSTRATING COMPASSION

I am fascinated with the word "compassion" in Scripture. This word speaks volumes. It is the unique word which is only used when God and Jesus are in mind. It means "feelings toward the needy." The following is one occasion when it is used.

There was a father who waited and waited, watching the road (Luke 15:11-32). One of his only two sons had left his father and home to have a good time in a far country. Silly fellow. That father was a picture of our Heavenly Father. Day after day the father peered at the distant hill over which his boy might one day reappear. When the wonderful moment came, the father ran—*ran!*

I wonder if his running days were over until that moment? But love drove the father to get to that boy before his son had a chance to change his mind and turn away from home. The father took ten steps for every one the son took.

What a story! The greatest ever told, except for the story of Jesus Himself. There is so much in it. For instance, that son had been working among pigs, and had returned home in the only clothes he had, the dirty rags that still carried the stench of the pigsty. *But* the father "fell on his neck and kissed him"—embracing that smelly good-for-nothing! A profound affection and compassion overcame revulsion.

LOVE RESTORES RELATIONSHIPS

Is it so surprising that the older of the two sons disowned this unwashed tramp? He said to the father with a sneer, "This son of *yours* . . ." The reply he got was, "This *your* brother . . ." Love restores all relationships. *That's* the Gospel. The older brother accused the younger of wasting his money on prostitutes. This was his own supposition. It had not been mentioned before. But the father did not demand to know whether the allegation was true or false. He did not ask what his sins were. He only saw his son's plight. Here was a lost, dead man, needing to be loved back into life. It would take time, but he had *come back*. That was all the prodigal could do, and now the father could forgive. This provided a chance for restoration. And there is the Gospel, illustrating the word "Compassion."

I understood this story better when I realized that the word "compassion" implies a physical reaction. It has to do with the internal organs, when a feeling goes through our system and leaves us shocked inside. We say, "my stomach turned over," or, "my heart stood still." And that is the word used to describe the feelings which disturbed Jesus when He gazed upon the people. He was *moved* with compassion (Matt. 9:36). It was no mere condescending act of charity. It was the irresistible instinct of a mother or father snatching back a child from danger. In a sense, Jesus could not or would not help Himself. "He saved others; Himself He cannot save" (Matthew 27:42).

> *Jesus was moved with compassion. It was no mere condescending act of charity. It was the irresistible instinct of a mother or father snatching back a child from danger.*

That and that alone accounts for the fact that He troubled Himself with universal sicknesses and the sea of human ills so long accepted as an unalterable fact of life, ills seen sometimes even as the judgment of God. It is certainly true that many things resulted from Christ's miraculous healings of the sick: the glory of God, the confirmation of His divine Sonship. But that was not why He healed. His purpose in healing was *to heal*—simply that. I do not play the piano to prove that I have fingers, although that is also true, but because I love music. The purpose of music is music. The purpose of goodness is goodness. The consequences are mere side effects, quite incidental to His reason.

What could Jesus gain from His works of mercy? He did not need them for his own profit. Why did He go to Bethesda among that litter of humanity, who were like flotsam and jetsam cast up on a forgotten shore? Why should He go to Nain to meet a dead man, or go anywhere or come to earth at all, for that matter? There was no possible benefit or profit to Himself. The truth is, Jesus had a fatal attraction for the wretched. It led Him to a cruel death, but that was no consideration to Him. He would bring His healing touch to broken lives no matter what. We read that in the eyes of Jesus, the multitudes were as sheep without a shepherd and, "He was moved with compassion for them, and healed their sick" (Matt. 14:14).

Then he called His disciples and sent them out to do a similar work. His work became their work—to show compassion. It was his compassion delivered by the disciples. But did they feel it? Do we? The disciples came back excited and thrilled because they discovered they had power, and that devils were subject to them (Luke 10:17). They did not mention those who had been delivered, and never referred to any satisfaction it gave them that precious men and women now were free.

Jesus had a fatal attraction for the wretched. It led Him to a cruel death, but that was no consideration to Him. He would bring His healing touch to broken lives no matter what. We read that in the eyes of Jesus.

If we are disappointed when the afflicted remain afflicted, so is Jesus. In fact, we would not feel like that at all if He did not Himself, for He made us that way. He heals to alleviate the consequences of sin, forgiving also the sin, for the same reason He saves. In no other way could He be satisfied. Deep satisfaction to the Lord is loving, caring, saving, healing. He gets nothing else out of it.

A FURNACE OF LOVE

God is a consuming fire. He is all love, a furnace burning for His creatures. Whenever we carry the Gospel, it must be because we care. We are not to heal for the sake of seeing a wonder. God is not in show business. He didn't come on earth to make a name for Himself. If He did, His audience only made a nail for Him.

He made trees, and men stripped them of their grace and turned them into an ugly cross to exhibit Him for their derision. He created man and thus Judas Iscariot. The wood that bore Him, the iron that pierced Him, the Judas that betrayed Him—He made them in the beginning, knowing full well what their uses would be. But He still made trees and He still made iron for human benefit, whatever the eventual cost to Himself.

GROUNDLESS LOVE

Our own motives must be His. The love of God shed in our hearts by the Holy Spirit makes it possible. He loves us to love others. There may be imperfect motives behind our ministry. In the end, our work will be tested as by fire, and what was a performance for self will be hay, wood and stubble, instead of the gold and silver jewelry of love (1 Cor. 3:12-13).

> *God is a consuming fire. He is all love, a furnace burning for His creatures.*

Do you perhaps hanker for miracle power, for display? There is the occasional "demon hunter" who seeks exhibition opportunities. Do you want to be known as a person of prayer, or of great faith or super spirituality? Jesus said such people have already had their reward (Matt. 6:2).

Love cannot have reasons. It is the ultimate. When God spoke to Israel, He said He had loved them for no reason. It was not because they were a great nation, for they were smaller even than the peoples to be driven out of Canaan. The Lord told them He loved them because of His love for them— which is no reason at all! The reason for love is love, which is God Himself (Deut. 7:7-8). Love is not God, but God is love.

Jesus amazes me. He healed the man at the pool of Bethesda and went away and never even said who He was. What advantage did that healing bring Him? No glory, no fame—in fact, it brought Him trouble and persecution (John 5). He took a deaf man and led him by the hand outside the village so nobody would see him perform the miracle. He did the same with a blind man. He restored others and told them not to say a word. There is only one explanation for His entire work, and that is that He loved people.

PROFOUND COMPASSION

To have Christ's ministry is possible, but only to the degree of His compassion. A final consideration struck me. When Jesus stood at the tomb of Lazarus, why was it that He wept? I thought, "But surely He knew there was going to be that greatest miracle, a resurrection? He ought to have had a radiant face!" But instead we read, "He groaned in the spirit and was troubled." He even wept. Then the Jews said, "'See how He loved him.' Then Jesus, again groaning in Himself, came to the tomb" (John 11:33-38).

> *To have Christ's ministry is possible, but only to the degree of His compassion.*

Why? The answer is that Jesus saw in this scene of sorrow the agony of all bereavements. Death did not merely affect His friend Lazarus. It was not for His own circumstances that He showed such deep feeling. "He had no tears for His own griefs but sweat drops of blood for mine," wrote songwriter Charles H. Gabriel. Jesus saw every funeral at that moment, and the king of terrors that haunt mankind with death. It was because He possessed this profound compassion that He went down into the caverns of death and conquered it.

This is the Love, the Gospel and what we the Church, are all about. This is the Gospel the world awaits.

Chapter 11

THE ANOINTED
UNPROFESSIONAL

There is a Bible episode we heard over and over again when we were children. We have heard it until we think that it is only "kid's stuff," but it contains some of the most powerful words from God in all of Scripture. It is the story of the confrontation between David and the giant warrior, Goliath as told in 1 Samuel, chapter 17.

We must remember that we do not learn God's lessons with the head only. Our IQ has nothing to do with our spirituality. David had discovered truths as a mere lad. He was one of God's inspired spiritual geniuses. There are general truths in this account of the amazing performance of David in the Valley of Elah. Here are key elements that are the very spears and swords of spiritual battle. We see that Christian work and warfare are illustrated in this famous episode. These are the truths by which victory is possible. They are not David's secrets, but the secrets of the Lord of Hosts.

I do not pretend that these points are hard to discern. Merely to name the factors involved is not enough, though. I can do that right now. David's power lay in two equally important elements—faith and the anointing. But we cannot just leave it at that.

There are four kinds of people in this account, and I will make labels to identify them:

The Anointed Unprofessional - David
The Unanointed Professional - Israel's worrying warriors
The Ex-anointed Professional - King Saul
The Anti-anointed Professionals - Goliath and
the Philistines

THE ANOINTED UNPROFESSIONAL

David was not a professional warrior, but he was an anointed man. He didn't belong to the army of Israel. He didn't have anything to do with it at all. Scripture makes a point of telling us this. His job was back at home, minding sheep. He gate-crashed the whole army, an act of breathtaking audacity. But his anointing from God was his credential to do what he did. Actually, David originally only came to take a special treat from his dad and deliver a food hamper to his big brothers.

The anointed David, amazingly, was at this point an errand boy—an anointed errand boy. The Lord's anointed should be willing to be errand boys. If we are faithful in that which is least, the Lord will make us rulers over much. The anointing of God can rest on the humblest of workers.

David probably had never seen a battle or a battlefield, before he arrived in the valley of Elah. He came with anointed vision and boundless faith in the Lord. Among the men of the army of Israel however, he found only worrying warriors. Faith and victory were notably missing from the spirit of the army. He sensed grief and calamity.

The moment he opened his mouth to ask a question, he bumped into his eldest brother Eliab. David was a 17 year-old youngster and Eliab was a professional, a captain in the army. Eliab was also the man Samuel had *not* anointed. He was an unanointed professional. He represented the whole army of unanointed professionals, and who knows how many today believe they are in God's army? Incidentally, Eliab had faith—of a kind, but that we shall see later.

There was bound to be friction between the anointed and the unanointed. David was like sandpaper to Eliab, irritating. I want to point out some differences between these two classes, the Eliabs and the Davids.

WHERE THE ANOINTED
AND THE UNANOINTED DIFFER

David saw Goliath and heard the blasphemies that came out of his mouth. Eliab listened with a sinking heart. Something different happened to David, though. The anointing of the Lord began to heat up within him. At that same moment, the hearts of Israel's unanointed professionals became ice-cold with fear. This has always been a notable distinction between the two, and it is still so today. Anointing gives great boldness, making people fearless. The anointing makes the difference between an academic faith and a burning faith. Let me warn you—the one faith will always irritate the other. Don't be surprised. It's the old, old story.

Eliab mentally put himself next to Goliath for comparison and saw him as an awesome giant. David, in contrast, was a man of active faith and mentally put Goliath next to the God of Israel and saw the Philistine as a midget.

Eliab undoubtedly had reason on his side. But it left him weighing up the balance of Israelite and Philistine forces. He saw no other resources. Eliab was able to make professional assessments of battle situations, and he saw that Israel had no chance of winning. This professional officer mentally put himself next to Goliath for comparison and saw him as an awesome giant. David, in contrast, was a man of active faith and mentally put Goliath next to the God of Israel and saw the Philistine as a midget. Isn't it amazing what transpires when faith and fear are contrasted? David knew he had the Lord on his side, and felt holy stirring and indignation within his soul. That was because of the anointing which gave him resources unknown to others. His inner eyes of faith were upon Jehovah. God's anointing upon him made him hungry for victory, excited by his eager anticipations. He did more than just hope and pray. That anointing was the "guarantee" of things to come.

On the battlefield of faith it is not even necessary to "study your enemy" as some suppose. It is true that 1 Samuel 17 gives a detailed description of the weights and sizes of Goliath's weapons. This however was not what the anointed unprofessional David studied and considered; it was what the unanointed professionals studied. It was a neat piece of intelligence on the enemy, but it did not help them one bit. Even if Goliath had been one hundred times stronger than he was, it would not have influenced or intimidated David—he knew that His God could do anything!

> *Even if Goliath had been one hundred times stronger than he was, it would not have influenced or intimidated David—he knew that His God could do anything!*

Eliab was certainly a smart man. He had impressed even Samuel, the prophet. At first Samuel had thought that this man would make a fine king, but the Lord had said, "Do not look at his appearance or at the height of his stature, because I have refused him" (1 Sam. 16:7). Why? We shall see.

In human eyes, David was not worth consideration—just the youngest, a lively teenager. The kind that we might hesitate choosing to even give out the hymn books. But the Lord said, "Arise, anoint him; for this is the one!" A reddish-faced, unknown lad from the tribe of Judah. Being reddish suited the future king, as the jewel stone for Judah in the high priest's breastplate was red.

God's favor upon David had never given him favor with his seven unanointed brothers. Now, in the battle zone, Eliab spoke for all when he angrily asked David with whom he had left "those few sheep in the wilderness." David had not neglected his sheep. He had left them in the hands of a keeper. God's anointing does not allow anyone to neglect their proper duties. David was a man after God's own heart who did *all* God's will, even in the ordinary business of everyday duties. David, the anointed unprofessional, could not be bothered with Eliab's miserable quibbles—it was to him irrelevant nonsense.

The anointing of the Holy Spirit within him now reached the boiling point. To use a modern picture: David's faith was like a running engine and the anointing of God like a turbo-charger on top of it. He had to pull up the hand brake, as it were, so as to not jump on the enemy too soon. He ignored all mere protocol. If there was nobody to face Goliath

> *The army considered David an outsider, but he was God's insider, nevertheless.*

then he, a nobody, would face him. He would do it in the Name of the Lord, because he knew that the God of Israel was incapable of inaction! The army considered David an outsider, but he was God's insider nevertheless.

FACE TO FACE WITH THE EX-ANOINTED

Perhaps David overstepped the bounds by questioning the army's policy. But the long and the short of it was that he found himself in the tent of King Saul. Maybe it was a misunderstanding, but he said it was about time somebody faced the champion from Gath. The anointing, even more than David's faith, had made him speak out.

David recognized Goliath as his own enemy, not just as the army's target for the day. Here was the deadly foe of every man, woman and child in the land. Getting rid of him was everybody's business, army or no army.

That is true of the devil today. The Kingdom of God can't be run only by professionals paid out of church funds. Anointed unprofessionals are needed. The devil is a menace to everyone.

The ex-anointed had become the opinion leader of the unanointed— and nothing is more fatal than such a combination.

A battle needs supplies and money, some of which David had come to bring, although dollars are no substitute for dedication. But David could not stand around any longer. For what was he anointed? Everyone knew something should be done, but who would do it? Eager hands pushed David forward. No doubt Goliath would make mincemeat of him, but it would break the deadlock. A nobody like David didn't matter. He could be offered as the sacrificial lamb. Then Israel could get on with the main battle. Let us now enter the tent of King Saul and see what happened.

It was obviously a joke to Saul and to his generals when a raw lad from the country came in and proposed to be the defender of Israel. But the fact is, when Samuel the prophet had anointed the shepherd boy David, King Saul had become the ex-anointed of the Lord. Now the anointed and the ex-anointed stood face to face, eye to eye. Saul looked at David with amusement. But David was quivering under a powerful Holy Spirit anointing. The ex-anointed had become the opinion leader of the unanointed—and nothing is more fatal than such a combination. Saul said, "You can't fight Goliath! Do you know what you are up against? Have you seen how big he is? You don't know the first thing about combat. He has been a warrior all his life."

There are always those trying to push others out, and always those trying push others in to do what they don't fancy doing themselves. Eliab wanted to freeze David out, but you can't freeze fire. Saul wanted David to go in and fight instead of himself. If the army had voted, they would have been 99.9 percent against David—I say 99.9 percent because I believe that David would have voted for himself—but David wasn't waiting to be democratically elected, nor was he thinking about popularity. Jesus said, "How can you believe, who receive honor from one another?" (John 5:44).

THE EX-ANOINTED

Now, the captain of all the ex-anointed is the Ex-anointed Satan, who once was "the anointed cherub who covers." This is quite an awesome fact, as we read in Ezekiel 28:14-17:

> You were the anointed cherub who covers; I established you; you were on the holy mountain of God; you walked back and forth in the midst of fiery stones. You were perfect in your ways from the day you were created, till iniquity was found in you. . . . Your heart was lifted up because of your beauty, you corrupted your wisdom for the sake of your splendor; I cast you to the ground.

And Isaiah writes:

> How you are fallen from heaven, O Lucifer, son of the morning! . . . For you have said in your heart: "I will ascend into heaven, I will exalt my throne above the stars of God; . . . I will be like the Most High." (Isaiah 14:12-14)

Really, in a sense, the devil had faith. According to James, "Even the demons believe—and tremble!" (James 2:19). But the anointing had departed from Satan and left the evil husk of a once-illustrious being.

Now King Saul was a pathetic reflection of the same condition. Just as Satan would pursue Jesus to kill him, Saul soon would be pursuing the anointed David. In both cases, a kingdom was at stake. *The ex-anointed will always persecute the anointed of the Lord.* Satan, considered it robbery to be equal with God (compare Phil. 2:6), but Jesus who "being in the form of God" did not. "But," the Apostle Paul continues: "[He] made Himself of no reputation, . . . He humbled Himself and became obedient to the point of death, even the death of the cross. Therefore God also has highly exalted Him and given Him a Name that is above every name" (Phil. 2:7-9). Praise be to God for Jesus!

When David met Saul, he was undaunted. He had certainly never fought a professional soldier, but he had fought wild beasts. Predators were always after his flock. A bear and a lion had come and wished they hadn't when they met David. Goliath was a one-man war machine, a human tank, but in David's view he was too big a target to miss, and with God, David felt like a whole armored division. "For by You I can run against a troop, by my God I can leap over a wall" (Ps. 18:29).

With David it was all God—God or nothing. And it was God's honor Goliath challenged. Goliath had thrown down the gauntlet, not merely to men, or to the Israeli army. He had "defied the armies of the Living God" (1 Sam. 17:36). That was Goliath's mistake—a mistake, as it turned out for him, slightly more unhealthy than a headache, for he lost his head. All David had to do was—well, simply whatever had to be done. God would help David to succeed. Faith told him he could, and the anointing super-charged his eagerness to do so.

SAUL'S ARMOR

Now Saul should have fought Goliath. We are told he was head and shoulders above the biggest men in Israel. Furthermore, he was the king, the one who had known the Lord's anointing. And there was also mighty Abner. Instead, the two of them let David do it. In fact, the first thing Saul did, like unanointed professionals often do, was to make sly fun of this peasant lad who believed God could give him victory over the greatest warrior in the Philistine forces. In Saul's mind, David was naive. David, a deliverer? That was just absurd.

So King Saul smiled, winked at his brave general staff, and offered David the use of his own royal armor. That would be comical. What a figure David would cut, half Saul's size, parading in front of two armies in that oversized equipment!

First, the leather coat. The shoulders, with layers of leather and bronze, stood out six inches from David's body, burying him. The chain mail weighed him down. The bronze helmet—David turned his head sideways and the helmet stayed forwards. The belt was Size 44—David's waist was only 29 inches. Saul's sword was so long that it trailed on the ground and threatened to trip little David. Goliath would die, all right—of laughter!

WHEN THE ANOINTING BOILS . . .

What must have been the reaction of Goliath? "Give me a man," he had roared (1 Sam. 17:10). He had waited for Israel's answer. It would have to be their greatest man of war, he surmised. Then, the hero finally came, emerging from the ranks of Israel's mighty warriors. Goliath could hardly believe his eyes when, with an uproar on both sides, a stripling in sandals and a shepherd's tunic ran across the field! His weapons were a couple of staves and a little sling. Goliath felt it was a studied insult—did Israel think they were only chasing off a dog, sending a lad with sticks and a sling?

Don't mistake presumption for faith, and remember, to do God's work, you must have God's anointing. It is no coincidence that the only believer in the army to tackle the enemy was the one who carried the anointing of God.

David's faith might have been evident in his being there at all. But Goliath also was up against the very Spirit of God. Invisible within the shepherd lad's heart, the anointing began to boil. There was no holding back any longer. Note that 1 Samuel 17:48 says that David "ran" toward the Philistine champion, like an arrow released from the bow of the Almighty God. The unanointed professionals watched from a safe vantage point.

Goliath bellowed a hoarse warning at David. In contrast came the voice of the sweet singer of Israel, the musical tenor who later soothed Saul in his mad fits. Maybe Eliab or some other scornful men shouted, "Sing to him, David—he might cry and go home." The words didn't soothe Goliath.

Anyway, Israel's thousands were on their feet, watching and shouting. The soldiers had done a lot of shouting. They were good at it. Rattling their spears on their shields, hundreds of them made a frightening racket altogether. But Goliath was one of those stubborn facts that would not go away.

Mind you, if it was a matter of faith, all the army had faith. David believed nothing more than they did. They had the Ark of the Covenant. Not only that, but the Israelites were God's chosen people. They sang about it. Chanted a Psalm, even— "The Lord mighty in battle." They stamped it out in rhythm until the ground shook. All that, but still nobody did any fighting. They had faith, but they did not act on it. The anointed David, however, felt the Spirit of God shaking him.

The army of the Lord—is it like that today? Does His army do everything except fight? Everything except evangelize. Israel spent time organizing themselves—and that's all. They polished their weapons, argued about who should be the leaders,—no doubt discussed the army's structure, policy and methods. The army of the Lord can be like that, chiefly concerned with polishing up the wherefores and therefores of their constitution, discussing church order, claiming to be "a people of power," like Israel facing Goliath. But they do nothing actually aggressive for God, no real evangelism.

GOD'S BULLET

David did what any of those men should have, and certainly could have, done. He fought. *Just that.* But note: he turned his passive beliefs into active faith. Because he *believed*, he tackled the giant. He did not use professional weapons, but only what he was accustomed to—a sling and a stone. With an expertise honed by

> *Know this—your word, if it is God's word, carries far more weight than all argument.*

years of stone-slinging while sheep-watching, David probably could have "hit a hair at 50 yards," but facing a giant was another situation.

Now here is the crux of the matter. Don't mistake presumption for faith, and remember, to do God's work, you must have God's anointing. It is no coincidence that the only believer in the army to tackle the enemy was the one who carried the anointing of God.

That is what God wants—men of faith and anointing. The anointed man will match his action to what he believes. That is the man whose faith will make him attempt the impossible, doing what he would never do unless he believed God.

We all can do the ordinary things and trust God. David did the extraordinary and trusted God. That is what faith can be like, when it comes with the anointing of the Spirit. We believe for the impossible—*and do it!*

I have no idea how hard a stone from a sling can hit. But I do know that when it is slung by an anointed slinger, it can travel like a bullet. That stone sank into Goliath's forehead, prostrating him, and the youthful victor administered the "coup de grace" with Goliath's own sword.

Know this—your word, if it is God's word, carries far more weight than all argument. It catches people where they are not protected. I rely upon it when preaching to thousands of people, all of whom are different. God knows best what Word will reach them. The professional enemy had prepared for every danger, but forgot to prepare for a stone from a sling. God has many a surprise to spring on the devil. He does not understand who, or what means, God is likely to choose. When we move in the Holy Spirit, we always will find the Achilles heel of the devil and thus defeat him.

The anointed unprofessional David stuck to his brand of active faith and gloriously succeeded. Then all the brave, unanointed professionals of Israel took heart. They chased the Philistines, who were fleeing already! That must be some other kind of faith!

FINALLY: THE ANOINTED PROFESSIONAL

It would be unfair not to mention the following. David soon became a "professional" as well—an anointed professional. Anyone who does something long enough will qualify at some time! But, in spite of relying upon higher learning or old routines and rites, he kept a spiritual freshness through the Holy Spirit, as God said in Psalm 132:17-18:

> "There I will make the horn of David grow; I will prepare a lamp for My Anointed. His enemies I will clothe with shame, but upon Himself His crown shall flourish."

The "lamp" was the Spirit of revelation, the Holy Spirit. David received new spiritual insight all the time. He relied upon the anointing of the Holy Spirit, and thus upon His Lord and God. God does not work miracles in order to save us trouble, but to glorify His Name.

Believe. Act. Make sure of your anointing and say to the Lord, as does the hymn writer, "Now bid me run, and I will strive with things impossible." God moves with the people who move!

Chapter 12

THE WEAPONS OF OUR WARFARE

Today we are seeing entire nations shaken by the power of God. What we saw God do, for example, in the West African nation of Togo was awesome. The entire country knew about our Gospel crusade in the capital city of Lome, because each night our meetings were the number one story on the national television news! What made it even more remarkable was that the crusade took place during the Gulf War, and yet reports about the lame walking and the blind receiving their sight took top billing.

While governments in the West become more cynical toward the move of God in the earth, this is not the case in Africa! More than once I have been privileged to address the Parliaments of African nations—what would be the equivalent in their countries to the American Congress. As an ambassador of Christ, I have not been ashamed to preach the whole Gospel and have given bold altar calls in these legislative halls. But I have not stopped with salvation. I have also prayed for the sick, and it never ceases to amaze me and my team when officials from the Prime Minister on down wait in line for the ministry of the laying on of hands! What a mighty God we serve! I have vowed never to limit God.

Of course, I'll be the first to admit that all of this is not man's doing, but the work of God. People do ask, "What is the secret of your success?" That, at least, is how they put it. The fact is that *nothing* can measure up to the effects of the Gospel.

This is my revelation, and it was Paul's also: the Gospel is the power! (Rom. 1:16). I have every confidence in the efficacy of the Gospel to save souls when salvation through Jesus Christ is clearly preached. And miracles will pop up like popcorn when we dare to preach that Jesus Christ is still the Healer.

The kind of evangelism that wins the world— Holy Spirit evangelism.

Entertainment, politics and other attractions may draw crowds, but nothing is magnetic like the Gospel. It offers no cheap popularity, yet its wonderful power is bringing millions together in marvelous fellowship all around the globe. But how does it happen? The answer is the kind of evangelism that wins the world—Holy Spirit evangelism.

Holy Spirit evangelism makes use of the weapons God has given for this task, namely the gifts of the Spirit. (The gifts of the Spirit are so important, so vital, as keys to winning the lost that I have written another book explaining the purposes of the gifts and how to flow in them.)

Anointed preaching, along with anointed music and singing, are not the only explanations for our success, I am sure. We must have something more as did the first disciples. The New Testament talks about magnificent manifestations, which were things to see. They are truths made visible.

What are the works of God? They are not only conversions, or even healings. They include revelation, prophecy, supernatural knowledge, wisdom, discernment, dreams, visions and authority over the powers of Satan. These are all aspects of our crusades and meetings which I feel have helped to attract the hundreds of thousands. People wake up to the reality of spiritual things when they see something that is beyond mere words. The gifts of the Spirit supply this slice of experience.

In this chapter I want to stress the glorious possibilities of these weapons, the gifts. By these God-given means, the timid soul can become bold, and the defensive person can become aggressive. The Lord intends us to carry the credentials of an ambassador. To those whom He sends, He also gives His startling power and authority.

Many believers desire spiritual gifts, but perhaps are nervous about using them. "Suppose I am wrong?" they reason. But the worst mistake is not to employ the weapons of the Lord. Remember some key Scriptures.

"Be strong and very courageous." (Josh. 1:7)

In the fear of the LORD there is strong confidence. (Prov. 14:26)

Be strong in the grace that is in Christ Jesus. (2 Tim. 2:1)

Desire spiritual gifts . . . and desire earnestly to prophesy. (1 Cor. 14:1,39)

Concerning the demonstration of spiritual gifts, there is an Old Testament passage that has fascinated me for a long time. Put alongside the New Testament truth, it gives a clear picture of how God does turn the tides and the tables on His enemies:

Then Joash the king of Israel came down to him [Elisha], and wept over his face, and said, "O my father, my father, the chariots of Israel, and their horsemen!" And Elisha said to him, "Take a bow and some arrows." So he took himself a bow and some arrows. Then he said to the king of Israel, "Put your hand on the bow." So he put his hand on it, and Elisha put his hands on the king's hands. And he said, "Open the east window"; and he opened it. Then Elisha said, "Shoot"; and he shot. And he said, "The arrow of the LORD'S deliverance and the arrow of deliverance from Syria; for you must strike the Syrians in Aphek till you have destroyed them." (2 Kings 13:14-17)

THE PITY PARTY AND THE PROPHET

The New Testament talks about magnificent manifestations, which were things to see. They are truths made visible.

Joash, the King of Israel, was young and inexperienced when a disaster threatened his kingdom. The Syrian army had mobilized against him, and he knew he could muster nothing to match it. He had terrifying visions of defeat and his own imprisonment. Even the possibility of death haunted him. He felt sick with worry. But wait! Wasn't there a man of God still around who could help him in his despair? As is often the case when backed against the wall, both president and pauper alike will make a pitch to God.

Joash was one of Israel's bad kings, but in the time of trouble he, too, remembered the Lord's prophet, Elisha.

The king decided to visit Elisha, who was now about eighty years old. He approached the elderly, dignified man with flatteries. He described Elisha's usefulness to Israel as like "the chariots of Israel and their horsemen!" Then he "wept over his face," letting the prophet see his tears, crying, "O, my father, my father . . . " It was quite a show!

The fact was, however, that Joash wasn't weeping because Elisha was dying, but because he might die himself.

Old Elisha, well-schooled in following the promptings of the Holy Spirit, gave the king what seemed to be strange instructions. He simply told the king to take his bow and arrows. (I think that he could just as well have said, "Take your handkerchief." Elisha had seen too much of Joash's ways to be moved by his sob story.)

God was not impressed, either. It is high time for somebody to say that God knows when people are weeping only because they feel sorry for themselves.

Some people seem to need much more of other peoples' time. In fact, it is often difficult to know what their trouble is, if indeed they know themselves. They may occasionally be victims of mental bruising earlier in life. But leaders who specialize in counseling may find such patients give them plenty of practice. There is the danger that the hours devoted to their pity parties could drive the trouble deeper into their consciousness, even making such folk feel they are very special sufferers, beyond the normal ability of the Lord to help them. But nothing is too hard for God.

Our job is not to "coddle" Christians who already may feel too sorry for themselves. Our aim is to wake them up, not give them a sedative! People need to come out of themselves and to see again the needs of a dying world.

Our job is not to "coddle" those Christians who already may feel too sorry for themselves. Our aim is to wake them up, not give them a sedative! People need to come out of themselves and to see again the needs of a dying world. Beware! This is a wearing down tactic of the devil: devoting valuable time to people who never resolve their personality problems. Precious time spun in circles of talk could have been invested in winning the lost.

Well, Elisha was exercising the gift of the discerning of spirits. He also had a word of wisdom. He had no time to supply tissues for the king's eyes when national calamity loomed. He resorted to no probing inquiries. The need was plain. By the word of the Lord, therefore, without formalities for the royal presence, Elisha came straight to the point.

"Take bow and arrows." He was brusque, perhaps, but when enemies are invading, the answer had to be just that—bow and arrows. A military mind-set was needed. Joash must forget himself and play the man.

TREMBLING OR TRIUMPHANT
SAINT?

Many churchmen and medical doctors have opposed divine healing. They have made much of those who are "disappointed" and who are not immediately healed. They have conveniently forgotten that doctors disappoint millions. Nearly everyone in the graveyard had been to a doctor first.

Where are our weapons? Paul wrote, "Stir up the gift of God which is in you (2 Tim. 1:6). He instructed, "Stir up." The word Paul used has to do with fire, just as you would stir up a campfire, and it means "to kindle," "to bring up to full flame." Don't cool off! Stir up that fire! Use the fan on the dying embers.

Joash was a feeble king, as we shall see, with little fire in his bones. He went crying to Elisha, "my father, my father" when he was scared, instead of mustering his army and bringing weapons out of the armory. Elisha would have appreciated action a lot more.

We have our weapons, and the devil has done his best to stop Christians from using them. When the Pentecostals opened God's armory at the beginning of this century, nearly the entire Church rose up in alarm. Until then, preachers too often had relied on human means, and not on the power of the Holy Spirit.

Many churchmen and medical doctors have opposed divine healing. They have made much of those who are "disappointed" and who are not immediately healed. They have conveniently forgotten that doctors disappoint millions. Nearly everyone in the graveyard had been to a doctor first, yet nobody would be so foolish as to demand the closing of all hospitals! Some church folk object to divine healing simply because some are not healed, and so do not minister to the sick at all. This leaves everybody unhealed! Where is compassion, or obedience to the Scriptures?

Other gifts also have come under attack. When the "word of knowledge" was first being restored by Pentecostal and charismatic evangelists, many declared its workings to be "like spiritualism." Why shouldn't God do such mighty things? In fact, spiritualism and clairvoyance are only the devilish counterfeit of what God means to do. The gifts of the Holy Spirit are far greater than anything the occult can manufacture. There must be the real wherever there is the false.

Some Spirit-filled people have let their bow and arrows (their gifts, their spiritual weapons) gather dust in a corner because of critics. Others have been hurt, perhaps by remarks from a fellow believer, and thus have dropped their gifts of prophecy, or tongues and interpretation. They have "lost" them, though God never reclaims them, for "the gifts and the calling of God are irrevocable" (Rom. 11:29). These gifts *must be* recovered.

Hear the word of the Lord: Go back to the day and to the place where you left those spiritual gifts, and ask the Lord to forgive you. Don't despair; the gifts are still there, albeit dormant. Dry your tears quickly and "take bow and arrows"— *again!*

WAITING FOR GOD'S MOMENT

When I enter a meeting, I carry my bow and arrows with me. The bow is already under tension, for I am praying in my heart, "Lord, which is your appointed target? Where is the word of knowledge? In which direction is the anointing of the Holy Spirit flowing? Where is the key miracle for today?" That is what I mean when I say that my bow is under tension. I'm poised to shoot as the Holy Spirit commands!

King Joash was a pathetic character. Surely trained as a warrior, he nevertheless did not readily take up his bow and arrows. He couldn't see properly, because of all his unmanly weeping. He was so scared by the enemy's threat that his hands shook. But then, something wonderful happened that changed everything.

Elisha put his hands upon the king's hands. This is a comforting picture of how God takes over for us. After all, it is not us operating the gifts of the Spirit, but the hand of God upon us. For example, Ezra kept repeating that, "The good hand of his God [was] upon him" (Ezra 7:6,9,28; 8:18). And Ezra wasn't the only one strengthened. The Bible is full of testimony of those "strong in the Lord and in the power of His might" (Eph. 6:10). Glory to God! It is exciting.

Having the gifts, God's bow and arrows, is one thing. Using them is another. "Prophets" should not just open their mouths because they are prophets. There is God's moment of command, that touch of God upon the hand.

In Africa, there is a charming story of an elephant who found the nest of an ostrich. The mother ostrich had gone off for a drink at the river. The elephant saw the exposed eggs, and big elephant tears rolled down her trunk. "How can a mother be so irresponsible and leave her eggs unprotected? Well, until she returns, I will help out." So the elephant, with maternal concern, sat on the nest. The devastating result, of course, was scrambled eggs. Are some Christians like that?

Elisha's touch imparted strength. The king dried his eyes, and fear left him. Divine confidence came. That same experience can be ours. It has been mine very many times. Suddenly, I will know that the enemy is defeated. I am sure miraculous things will take place. The anointing is there, breaking the yoke. We can be strong in strength which God supplies through His eternal Son.

"OPEN THE WINDOW"

Elisha next told Joash, "Open the east window." So you have the weapon gifts, you have the anointing. Now what? You can't shoot arrows through a closed window, so open it, begin to prepare and make opportunity. Set things up. Clear the decks for action. What I mean is, listen to the Holy Spirit in this matter, as Joash listened to Elisha. It may mean pushing aside normal arrangements, "official channels" and even courtesies perhaps, but if God says it, do it—while always remembering the elephant and the ostrich! When Jesus speaks, don't let anyone stop you.

I was about fifteen years old when God first put His Hands on mine and used me in a special way. I was in a prayer meeting in a church in northern Germany where my father was the pastor. We were all kneeling when the power of God came over me, and I felt as if my hands were filled with electricity. I clearly heard the Lord tell me, in my heart, "Arise and lay your hands upon Sister C."

I nearly passed out thinking of the consequences, for my father was a very strict man. How could I just get up and put my hands on that lady? But when I hesitated, the Lord seemed to turn up the voltage, and I felt as if I were dying. Slowly, I lifted my head and peered around for Sister C. I crept as low to the floor as I could so I wouldn't be detected. Then I quickly popped up and put my hands on her head. At that moment I felt the power of God go through my hands into her body.

Father had seen me, however, and his face showed he was not pleased. He went straight to her.

"What was Reinhard doing to you?"

"Oh!," she replied, "When Reinhard laid his hands on me, it was as if electricity flowed through my body, and I am healed!"

By going to her as God commanded, I learned this lesson: "Open the window." When Joash had done that, the next command could be given.

SHOOT!

> *The arrows of God are self-targeting, and they will never miss! They are like preprogrammed cruise missiles. They will strike, and no heart can evade them.*

Interestingly, Elisha did not say, "Take aim!" There was nothing for which to aim. God wanted him simply to shoot! I find this extremely comforting: The arrows of God are self-targeting, and they will never miss! They are like preprogrammed cruise missiles. They will strike, and no heart can evade them. Isn't this a wonderful discovery? When you take this principle on board, you will say, "What have I been waiting for? Perfection? Three degrees behind my name like the alphabet?" All that God wants us to do is to obey.

For example, when God gives a word of knowledge, I need not try to figure out whether it fits, or whether it is likely to be correct. God knows better than we know. My duty is to release the arrow from the bow, and it will become an "arrow of deliverance." The Spirit of God alone can plumb the depths of a man's own spirit. God will not slip up. The Spirit is familiar with everybody's history and with their most secret thoughts. For our rational minds, it is not always easy just to shoot through an open window of opportunity without seeing the actual target. When one does, though, the results are amazing. As the song by John H. Sammis says, "Trust and obey, for there's no other way to be happy in Jesus, but to trust and obey."

One of the overwhelming experiences I had of this kind involved my brother. We had grown up together as sons of godly parents, but he didn't want to follow Jesus. When we became adults, he had his career and life mapped out.

Time passed, and I didn't know that his wife had left him and that his best friend had died of cancer. His life had become meaningless to him. Then one night he had a vivid dream. He seemed to be walking on a high bridge when he slipped and felt himself falling, crying out. He awoke, drenched in perspiration.

Later he said, "For the first time in my life, I had a burning desire to pray to God, remembering the Scripture I had learned as a child, 'Call upon me in the day of trouble; I will deliver you' (Psa. 50:15). I went down on my knees and said, 'Lord, You know that I do not even know that You exist, but my brother Reinhard is your servant. Give me a sign through him that You are alive.'"

That night, I was six thousand miles away in South Africa. I didn't know about his troubles, nor that he was considering ending his own life, for there was very little communication between us. However, in the small hours of the morning, I had a terrible dream myself. I also saw a high bridge and my brother walking on it in some kind of fog. The bridge had no guard rails, and I feared that he might lose his orientation and fall off. He walked on, into that fog. I dreamed that I called out his name in desperation. Then, the next sound heard was that of a voice crying out from the bottomless depths. It was my brother's voice.

I woke up, wet with perspiration, and asked, "Lord, what is this?" He answered me, "Your brother is on the bridge to eternity. If you do not warn the Godless, I will require his blood from your hands." The fear of God came upon me. In brief, I wrote a letter to him. True, I had fierce battles in my own heart before doing so, but I told him of my dream. Also, I pleaded with him to receive Jesus Christ as his personal Savior.

One day before Christmas in 1987, I received his reply. Jesus had wonderfully saved his soul. Hallelujah! He knew his sins were forgiven. He wrote, "I am walking with the Lord every day. He has solved all my problems." When I received that letter, I could not control my emotions, and I just wept for joy.

How wonderful the Holy Spirit is! How effective are His gifts! They are God's powerful weapons. We play into the devil's hands when we are shy about them or apologetic about their use. What if I had not written that letter? What if I never had opened the east window, shooting that arrow into the dark? I did not do it led by my rational decision, but the arrow nonetheless found its mark.

In the Name of Jesus, I say to you, *open your window! Push aside your fears!* Let your obedience in faith overrule all your nervousness. Let go and let God have His wonderful way through you! And let your wisdom be: "The wisdom that is from above [which] is first pure, then peaceable, gentle, willing to yield, full of mercy and good fruits, without partiality and without hypocrisy" (James 3:17).

JOY!

The men and women whom God uses . . . have moved out of religious routine into the winds of the Holy Spirit.

When Joash shot that arrow through the casement, something happened to Elisha. He shouted, "The arrow of the LORD'S deliverance and the arrow of deliverance from Syria; for you must strike the Syrians at Aphek till you have destroyed them" (2 Kings 13:17). Joash believed it, and went forth in the strength of that confidence. Three times he overcame the Syrians, recovering his lost cities of Israel.

One mighty meeting with God changed the course of that king. That is all it takes, one meeting with God. The men and women whom God uses have had such a meeting with God. They have moved out of religious routine into the winds of the Holy Spirit. One can have that meeting, but you have to be desperate enough to break through. The essential thing is the anointing of God. Until you have that, all else is presumption. When you have His orders, it is presumption *not* to obey.

BOILING POINT

The story of Joash and Elisha is remarkable. What happened, as I have described here, gives us these great truths. But the fact is, there is still another facet to it. Joash could have done even better. We go on to read that the prophet Elisha told him to take his arrows now and "Strike the ground." He did, three times, only half-heartedly. "The man of God," we read, "was angry with him, and said, 'you should have struck five or six times; then you would have struck Syria till you had destroyed it! But now you will strike Syria only three times'" (2 Kings 13:19).

Despite the prophet's hand on his, the king's weak-willed character revealed itself. Joash was not bold. Just three inspired knocks on the ground was typical of a hazy, lazy temperament. A man of powerful intentions would have done even that small job well, and would have struck the ground thoroughly time after time, giving it a good hammering.

God loves vigorous souls who put everything they have into what they do, however small the command. No command of God is a matter of unimportance. "Whatever your hand finds to do, do it with your might" (Eccl. 9:10). What you are doesn't show just in the big battles, but in the little ones as well. You won't kill Goliath if you run away from a bear or a lion.

God can do so much for you, if you give yourself *wholly to Him and to His commands*. "Whatever He says to you, do it" (John 2:5).

The essential thing is the anointing of God.
Until you do have that, all else is presumption. When you have His orders, it is presumption not to obey.

Consider Joseph.   In Potiphar's home, in prison, or in charge of Egypt's harvests, he put everything he had into his job.   That was the way he became master of Egypt.   Do what you can, when you can, and all you can, wherever you are, and God will make you ruler over much.

When I laid my hands on that sick sister in my father's prayer meeting, I was given a glimpse of something important.   The gifts of the Spirit are not to be reserved for some future occasion, but are to be used today.

With the hand of God upon you, "Take up the bow and arrow! Open the window! SHOOT!"

Part IV

Success

Chapter 13

IMPOTENT OR IMPORTANT?

The sign of the Living Christ is an empty tomb, not an empty church. Back street missions are not the ideal for which Jesus died.

The Bible is a success story. The idea of a Gospel which doesn't make progress is the exact opposite to the Gospel we read of in the Word. The Bible sets before the Church a plan for advance in the face of all opposition and evil.

Some think a successful church, one that attracts all manner of people, can't be spiritual. What is our vision? God with His back to the wall? God as a charitable cause? A make-do church, always threadbare, merely scraping the bottom of the barrel?

From Genesis to Revelation, no such picture is found. God's servants went to the nations. They turned the tides of history. Paul caused Felix to tremble. He could say to the Roman Governor Festus, King Agrippa, Queen Bernice and numerous high officials, "this thing was not done in a corner" (Acts 26:26). Jesus challenged the whole of Israel and its rulers, and after He had ascended, the whole world faced the same challenge. Paul witnessed before the Emperor Nero himself.

Is your God a nonentity? Is He impotent? Or is He important and omnipotent?

My God is not the God of a little ghetto of believers that nobody need take any notice of. The God to serve is the great I AM, the One who humbled Pharaoh.

The Bible is a success story. The idea of a Gospel which doesn't make progress is the exact opposite to the Gospel we read of in the Word. The Bible sets before the Church a plan for advance in the face of all opposition and evil.

We have seen plenty of opposition in this world. The devil reigned unchallenged in some areas. We have met head-on all sorts of antagonism, false religion, witchcraft, crime and sin in all its variety. But the Gospel has battered the devil. Multitudes beyond number have started to follow the conquering King Jesus. Governments have supported our Gospel crusades, and at times have even given us official police escorts from airports and to the crusade sites. In three different countries I was invited to address the Houses of Parliament.

In the next set of chapters, I desire to encourage the expectation of blessing for the work of God. Anything else would not be the Word of God. The Bible never offers us comfort for decline. God's servants are committed to triumph. As I often say, we are "condemned to victory." Pentecost *is* revival.

If you read the books of Exodus, Deuteronomy, Joshua, Samuel, Kings and Chronicles, you will discover the principles of success—and also those of failure. We will look to these Scriptures. First we will turn to Joshua, which ought to be called "The Book of Success," and then we will turn to the Scriptures concerning Jonathan, Joseph, Balaam and others.

Chapter 14

SEVEN STEPS TO SUCCESS

Some have wishes. Others like Joshua, have purposes. A whole generation of Israel wished, and died still wishing. They had a wishbone, but no backbone. Joshua turned "wishes" into land, cities, homes and possessions.

Unbelieving Israel whined and died in the wilderness. Believing Joshua wined and dined in rich Canaan, the Promised Land.

When God said, "Go," even after forty years, Joshua still had "get up and go!" His go had not gone. Within three days he went. Israel had given up. To them, the Promised Land was Fantasy Land. Then Joshua made the 450-year-old dream come true.

Once God had commissioned him, Joshua did not wait. The right moment had come, but then the right moment was always at once for Joshua. It was not a question of striking while the iron was hot, but of striking *until* the iron was hot. He did not wait for a special day. Joshua made the day an occasion. For forty years, Joshua had nurtured a victory just waiting to happen. It happened when he decided. The door of history swung open at his touch.

Let's look at the seven factors behind his success, set out in the first chapter of the Book of Joshua. *All the seven victory factors lay in his own heart, not in his circumstances.* That is the difference between what happens for some people and what does not happen for others. Success is in ourselves and God's Word, not in our circumstances.

The LORD spoke to Joshua the son of Nun, Moses' assistant, saying: "Moses My servant is dead. Now therefore, arise, go." (Josh. 1:1-2)

What a moment to go! It began with a funeral. The man who was supposed to lead them was dead—"*now go,*" the Lord instructed. If God had said, "Moses, my servant is dead, so you can't go now. You had better go back to Egypt," it could have been expected. It was a disastrous hour. However, such a time is the hour for God. He revels in doing things in disastrous hours, bringing life out of death.

And—Joshua! Moses was one of the half dozen greatest men of all time, brought up as a prince, a genius, a born leader, an organizer, a writer, a personality who carried with him the aura of God as no other man on earth. How could Joshua compare to this giant?   How would Israel react? Perhaps with, "Who does this Joshua think he is? Why, he was only Moses' servant! He lead us?!"

Moses should have led them into Canaan, but never did, for all his mental and spiritual stature. How could any lesser man do it? To Joshua, the answer was that he could do what Moses did not do, because Moses already had accomplished what Joshua could not have done. Since Moses had been before him and done his mighty work, Joshua now could take the land. Moses had done everything he could. If Joshua did not take the final step over into Canaan, he would fail Moses.

Great men have gone before us all. It would be easy to feel too small to take their places. People ask, "Where are the new Pauls and Peters, the present-day Luthers and Wesleys?" But God does not want those men today. He wants us—the way He made us.

Now it was Joshua's hour. He was the divinely designated man for Canaan. Just as Moses prepared the way for Joshua, those great ones of church history have made everything ready for us—for the final push before Jesus comes. We must not let them down.

Those brave ones who went before us fought for freedom, for the Bible, for truth, for the Holy Spirit. They have left us a heritage often won by blood. Their wonderful resources are now ours. We can take up where they left off. We, who may feel like midgets next to these men, can wave the torches of giants, remembering that Jesus said his followers would do "greater works" (John 14:12).

Christian giants did their job, and now we do ours. They did not evangelize the world, but they opened it up. Paul is dead, Livingstone is dead. God is saying to us, "Now arise, go in and possess the land." What they could not do, we can do! Hallelujah! The vision in their hearts is the vista before our very eyes—the world for Jesus Christ. We must cast off our feelings of inferiority. Some compare

> *Those brave ones who went before us fought for freedom, for the Bible, for truth, for the Holy Spirit.*

Christians today with Christians of the past. Always remember this: A man's greatness lies only in God in any age. That's why Joshua could do what Moses did not—because he had Moses' God.

Step 1

REALIZE YOUR GREATNESS IS IN GOD

Twice in the Bible this wonderful, all-inclusive statement is made which is absolutely pregnant with potentiality: "With God all things are possible" (Matthew 19:26; Mark 10:27). Note the preposition "with." To *you* all things are possible, *with* God.

What had God promised to Joshua? "Every place that the sole of your foot will tread upon I have given you," (Josh. 1:3).

Joshua did not ride into Canaan on the back of an Arabian stallion but marched upon the basis of the promises of God. God had not said it to Moses only. He had given the land to Abraham, Isaac, Jacob and Joseph. Israel inherited the promise. But that promise was not to be fulfilled for the physical descendants of these great men. Only those who were the "faith" descendants of Abraham could claim the Promised Land.

> *Always remember this: A man's greatness lies only in God in any age.*

One entire generation of the physical offspring of Abraham died on the wrong side of the border, in unbelief. Two men were true children of Abraham—Caleb and Joshua. The faithless all died in the wilderness— they had disinherited themselves. The two faith children lived and went in later—leading the believing second generation. How? They took the land by stepping on it. They were not content merely with the title deeds. They entered into their estate.

Step 2

ALL OF GOD'S PROMISES THAT WERE MADE TO OTHERS BECOME OURS BY FAITH

They are made-to-measure promises, tailored to our needs. They are as much for you as if God personally had appeared and spoken to you. Your only requirement is that you must put them on. The Lord's question was, and is, "There remains very much land yet to be possessed." The only land remaining to be possessed was what Joshua had made up his mind to have. It was theirs by faith. "Faith is the substance of things hoped for," (Heb. 11:1). Joshua had a vision, laid claim to it, and went ahead to get it.

> "From the wilderness and this Lebanon as far as the great river, the River Euphrates, all the land of the Hittites, and to the Great Sea toward the going down of the sun, shall be your territory." (Josh. 1:4)

We read in the Book of J...
today want visions for a thril...
mystical pleasure. That is not wha...
are given to change the world. ...
practical men, not mystics. Believing...
The stuff of their dreams is concrete subst...

We don't stumble onto success accidentally...
aim, a vision. Hope, one of the three great abid...
qualities, is created by vision. Faith makes hope fe...

Joshua's secret of success was that he was hungry for God's maximum. The boundaries described above have their own secret—they are expandable, encompassing anywhere from 135,000 to one million square miles. When God said, "the river Euphrates," its geographical position meant that Israel could extend to any point on the river—the border was expandable. It allowed for ever-increasing faith and ever-enlarging vision. God had given a rubber band-promise with a built-in elasticity which could satisfy even the boldest spiritually. Joshua's attitude was one of a man of faith.

> *God's true dreamers are practical men, not mystics. The stuff of their dreams is concrete substance.*

What a dream for Israel! After all, they were runaway slaves! Joshua dreamed dreams. Dreamers are the folks who change the world. Joshua was no longer a youth, and he anticipated the prophecy of Joel: "Your old men shall dream dreams," (Joel 2:28).

Dreams of world conquest for Christ are a Charismatic feature. That was the very vision which drove people to seek the power of Pentecost at the beginning of the Pentecostal Revival. That is what God sent the power to do.

el of dreams and visions. People
a supernatural experience, a
God intended. His visions
God's true dreamers are
dreamers are realists.
nce.

Joshua had an
ng Christian
sible.

D DO FOR
BOUT

ith Moses, so

leeply rooted
eliefs") some
nce is greater
with others.
of reasons to
sedly is. We
oly, or more
As if the pre-

*because He has
committed
Himself
irrevocably.*

sence of God depended upon us! But the promise of His Presence with us is unconditional.

From the beginning God said, "I will not leave you nor forsake you" (Josh 1:5). He made this promise to Joshua, and the same sentiment was repeated thirteen hundred years later in Hebrews 13:5, "I will never leave you nor forsake you."

God is with us not because we are good or because we have great faith. No such terms are laid down. He is with us because He has committed Himself irrevocably, as it were "for better for worse, for richer for poorer, in sickness and in health." "For your Maker is your husband," (Isaiah 54:5).

To judge whether He is with people or not, we go by the wrong signs. We look at this man or that and judge by what they accomplish or fail to accomplish. Does God shrink or swell according to the man or woman He is with? God is not more with an evangelist than He is with a pastor, or more with a pastor than He is with a church member. He is not more with a big church than with a little assembly, or more with Moses than with Joshua.

Moses had the most extraordinary experiences with God a man ever had. Joshua could not share these experiences fully at the time. But it was to Joshua that God said, "I will not leave you nor forsake you." The presence of God with us does not vary with our callings or with our successes. If God was only with us when we had success, success would never come!

People often say, "Why does God use that man? I could do what he does."

Exactly—you could! So why not start now and do what the other man is doing? How can He use you if you never do what that man does? That is why He doesn't use you.

A disgruntled employee stood by his boss's desk, complaining that he earned so much less than his boss. He said, "I could be sitting where you are. I am as good an engineer as you."

The boss retorted, "That's right, you could be sitting here. Why aren't you? I started this business with nothing, and you could have done the same."

Step 4

GO FORTH KNOWING GOD IS WITH YOU AS MUCH AS HE WAS WITH ANYBODY

Don't hang around for the right circumstances. God is your circumstance! He is with you. Others simply took advantage of this great circumstance, believed it and acted on it.

Joshua's name was originally "Hoshea" (salvation), but Moses added the divine Name to it, making "Jehoshua" (God who is salvation), or, in English, "Joshua." Your name, linked with God's Name, means something. You then can go forth in

the Name of the Lord with the same courage that God
drummed into Joshua:

Be strong and of good courage. (Josh. 1: 6)

Only be strong and very courageous. (Josh. 1: 7)

Be strong and of good courage; do not be afraid, nor be
dismayed. (Josh. 1: 9)

God emphasized courage to Joshua three times. After the
first time He gave the first reason: "I will be with you." The
second time He added "only": "only be strong and very
courageous."

On the third repetition He gave another reason: "Have I not
commanded you?" (Josh. 1:9). God commands, and that is
when God commends.

God gives us reasons for going forward. We can always
find reasons for holding back. Then we treat our fears as
virtues. We say, "I am not one to push myself." Or, "If God
wants me to do it, He will put me there." Or, "We must not
run in front of God." Or, "I am waiting for a clear leading
from God—we must not presume." Or, "I do not seek great
things for myself, but want to keep humble."

Meanwhile, men are dying. Are these honest or sufficient
reasons? Or is our fear holding us back? For everything
which the devil would throw at us to make us afraid, God has
given us something to counteract it. There are indeed causes
for our hesitations and nervousness. That is the natural thing.
But God calls us to a new life of adventure and daring. That
is the exhilaration of the Christian life. Paul said he was not
afraid to preach the Gospel at Rome. Maybe he was nervous
at the prospects, as he said he was at Corinth, "in fear, and in
much trembling" (1 Cor. 2:3). But he did not yield to his
feelings. He enjoyed the experience of God strengthening him
as he nearly single-handedly faced pagan Europe.

From the Scriptures, Paul learned how to handle fear. So must we:

Whenever I am afraid, I will trust in you. (Psalm 56:3)

The righteous are bold as a lion. (Prov. 28:1)

He spoke boldly in the name of the Lord Jesus. (Acts 9:29)

[Paul and Barnabas] speaking boldly in the Lord. (Acts 14:3)

He began to speak boldly in the synagogue. (Acts 18:26)

[Paul] spoke boldly for three months. (Acts 19:8)

They saw the boldness of Peter and John. (Acts 4:13)

"Lord . . . grant to Your servants that with all boldness they may speak Your word." (Acts 4: 29)

They spoke the word of God with boldness. (Acts 4:31)

These men were not super-humans who didn't know what fear was. They felt its quivering pangs. So did Elijah, whom James said was subject to like passions as ourselves. They conquered their fears, however. How? They remembered God had sent them. They obeyed and threw the responsibility to Him. "Have not I commanded you?" rang in their ears. In that case, why fear man, "whose breath is in his nostrils" (Isaiah 2:22)?

Paul never asked people to pray for him, that the power of the Spirit would rest upon him. He knew he had the anointing (Romans 15:29). God was with him. His prayer request was, "That utterance may be given to me, that I may open my mouth boldly to make known the mystery of the gospel, for which I am an ambassador in chains; that in it I may speak boldly, as I ought to speak" (Eph. 6:19-20). Note the "as I ought to speak." He was God's ambassador sent to speak.

Step 5

BE BOLD IN CHRIST

John Wesley said, "I am too afraid of God to be afraid of men." The fear of God casts out the fear of man. Jesus said, "Do not be afraid, only believe" (Mark 5:36). Literally, "don't have phobia, have faith." The opposite of fear is not courage, but faith:

> . . . Observe to do according to all the law which Moses My servant commanded you; do not turn from it to the right hand or to the left, that you may prosper wherever you go. This Book of the Law shall not depart from your mouth, but you shall meditate in it day and night, that you may observe to do according to all that is written in it. For then you will make your way prosperous, and then you will have good success. (Josh. 1:7-9)

That word contains every secret. You might read the most erudite books about the Bible. Scholarship is excellent, but: "The secret of the LORD is with those who fear Him" (Psa. 25:14). The hidden things of God—these are not known by the intellect. They are incommunicable. They rise and flower in our souls as we read the Word. The Bible is not a book of cryptic mysteries. It is plain enough, but only grasped by the hand of faith.

When Christ taught us to pray, "Give us this day our daily bread," He also meant the Word of God. Read it daily. The Father then will interpret it to us and feed our souls daily. The Bible is not for pedantics. Some want to correct others about phrases and words, but they miss the throb of God's heart altogether!

A preacher has one task: to preach the Word, as Paul said to Titus. Preach the Word, meditate in the Word at all times (*day and night*), get your message from the Word. Say what it says. Never be selective, adjusting the Gospel to suit the public palate.

You will never be short of ministry as long as you are full of the Word. Read it when you cannot study it. It is not the "deep things," dug up by going through a whole reference library, but the simplest statement which can set you on fire—and ignite others as well. Throughout the world, the need for Word ministry is only too apparent. There are preachers aplenty with stories, jokes, thoughts, psychology, charming speeches and good advice. Some have nothing to offer except a neat homiletical arrangement, nicely alliterated with correct introduction and denouement, like a beautiful frame with no picture.

> *The Word of God makes a man a prophet, not a mere pulpit performer.*

The Word of God makes a man a prophet, not a mere pulpit performer. Understanding of the Word is vital. Any man who gives himself to teaching and preaching this Word will find multitudes of hungry people waiting, like fledglings in a nest.

Most of all, the power of God is released through the preaching of the Gospel—Romans 1:16. Every time it is preached, it creates. It is a wonderful moment when the Holy Spirit acts, as He is bound to act. There is no need to prove Scripture. It will prove itself.

Step 6

"THIS BOOK OF THE LAW SHALL NOT DEPART FROM YOUR MOUTH" Joshua 1:8

If others are prosperous without it, do not follow them. For you, here is the real way—the Word, THE Word, and again THE WORD!

Within three days you will cross over this Jordan, to go
in to possess the land which the LORD your God is
giving you to possess. (Josh. 1:11)

*For you, here is
the real way—
the Word,
THE Word,
and again
THE WORD!*

This is what I like about Joshua—
he was immediate. Israel had been on
the east bank of the Jordan for an
entire generation. That river was not
very wide, but it may as well have
been the ocean. The other side was
only a legend of their fathers, a Cloud
Nine golden fancy, "the beautiful isle
of somewhere" and sometime.

Then one morning like any other, when it looked as if they
would be a tent city forever in the wilderness, the trumpet
sounded! The people were galvanized. The gates of history
swung open. "Prepare to enter the land in three days."

How many Christian dreams have been shelved, put aside
as too idealistic, for some indefinite future? God has no
indefinite futures. He gives commands and promises for
immediate realization. The Father knows the hour. The
revival everybody wants—now. Signs and wonders—now.
Bold going forth with the Gospel—now. Opening those new
churches—now.

They crossed Jordan and looked at the key city, Jericho.
Forty years before, twelve men of Israel, sent as spies, had
looked at the great walled cities of the Promised Land. Ten
brought back reports which discouraged the people. The cities
were, "Walled up to heaven," said the faithless spies in Deuteronomy 1:28 (KJV), and, as for the giants they saw there: "we
were like grasshoppers in our own sight, and so we were in
their sight" (Num. 13:33).

Never manifest a grasshopper mentality! God let the entire
population of Israel who were over twenty years of age wander
and die in the Wilderness because of their lack of faith. It

took forty years. As a man "thinks in his heart, so is he" (Prov. 23:7). If you think you are a grasshopper, you are! A man is what he believes. The only people who are little in God's sight are people little in faith—suffering from the grasshopper syndrome. In God you are not a grasshopper—ever.

Forty years before, two other spies, Caleb and Joshua, had viewed the land with eyes of faith and brought a good report. "The land . . . is an exceedingly good land. If the LORD delights in us, then He will bring us into this land and give it to us" (Num. 14:7-8).

Now the day Joshua longed for had come. The walls were still there, towering over all of them, just as the ten faithless spies had reported years before. But now Israel was inspired. They felt big enough to blow those walls down with the blast of a trumpet. They needed no dynamite. And blow them down they did. They walked around the walls for six days, with Jericho's inhabitants jeering, amused by such odd warfare. Then, on the seventh day, down the walls went. We are big, but only in God.

Step 7

GO IN NOW TO TAKE THE LAND

Israel did not just march and blow trumpets. When the walls fell, they went in, fought and took the city.

I want you to realize something vitally important: Long ago, the "walls of the city fell" so to speak, when Jesus said He saw Satan fall as lightning from heaven. "Now the ruler of this world will be cast out" (John 12:31). But that is not all that has to be done. We now go in over those fallen walls with the sword of the Word, to preach the Gospel and to take the city for God! Every wall has fallen in Jesus' Name. Now go and possess the land!

Chapter 15

POSITIVE INITIATIVE

"Find your gift and use it," the experts say. If you have a gift, take that advice. Don't bury your talent in the earth. But, this advice could be an excuse for some folk to settle back in their armchairs. They will profess that they have no gift.

The Bible has a better way: "Whatever your hand finds to do, do it with your might" (Eccl. 9:10). I take this to mean: Get into God's vineyard and leave no stone unturned.

Survey what has to be done, and get on with it. In some cases, the call of God is the need. If you look at whether you are gifted for a task or not, you might decide it doesn't lie within your province. You may leave it to someone else. It is the call of God and what needs to be done that matters.

We should not consult with ourselves about our gifts, for by faith God can lift us beyond ourselves and our limitations. It isn't you who does the work. It's God. Without Him, you can do nothing anyway. But you can do all things through Christ. We can walk on the water if need be, for all things are possible to him that believes.

What does God want you to do? The first thing He wants you to do, is not to spend years finding out what He wants. God keeps no one waiting for that long. If He wants a job done, there would be no point in keeping us guessing about it.

Faith in God makes the person! What we believe, we are. Don't undersell yourself to yourself. Selling yourself short is not humility, but a denial of the very purpose for which you were born. Here is a vital principle—the call of God must be obeyed if you want the power of God to work through you.

Remember that the great apostle Paul sat making tents— not planning intents. Faithful in the little things, God made him master of much.

What does God want you to do? The first thing He wants you to do, is not to spend years finding out what He wants. God keeps no one waiting for that long. If He wants a job done, there would be no point in keeping us guessing about it. Why should He do that? It would be ridiculous to hide from you what His purposes are for you. Nor will He make it terribly difficult for you to find out.

He always has a task at hand. It may not be a great task—it may be nothing heroic. Perhaps it is a job that you think is beneath your dignity, even one that could be considered menial. Remember that the great apostle Paul sat making tents—not planning intents. Faithful in the little things, God made him master of much.

Some are asking God to speak and guide them because they despise the day of small beginnings. They assume God has some great work for them and that it surely cannot be a little thing. "And do you seek great things for yourself? Do not seek them," said God through Jeremiah to his secretary/servant (Jer. 45:5). You can't steer a boat or a bicycle that isn't moving. God waits for you to move before He tells you which direction to take.

God does guide us. When Abraham's servant Eliezer found a bride for Isaac he said, "As for me, being on the way, the LORD led me" (Genesis 24:27). This is a divine principle. *You* take the initiative for God. That is how Paul went on his famous travels.

TAKE ACTION!

If there is a hole in the dam, plug it, don't pass a resolution about it. If a foe is breaking into the Promised Land, the demand is obvious. Fight! Don't wait! Don't ask God what to do, or study whether you have the gift. One man who either did not wait when he should, or did wait when he shouldn't, was King Saul. Doing nothing because we can't do something mighty is nothing but pride. But we have another lesson now, found in Chapters 13 and 14 of First Samuel.

THE WORST OF TIMES IS THE BEST OF TIMES

For centuries, there was competition between Israel and the Philistines for the land of Israel. The Philistines were the traditional enemies of Israel, both physically and spiritually. We can compare spiritual principles in that history to Christian work and warfare today. Constant Israeli-Philistine skirmishes took place, until David finally subdued the Philistines.

After Saul became King, he created a standing army of three thousand men, placing a third of them under his son Jonathan. At that time, the Philistines had the upper hand. They put garrisons here and there throughout the land of Israel, including one in the strategic pass from Bethel to Jericho, where the town of Michmash stood.

At this time, Jonathan had already made an attack on the Philistine forces, so now the Philistines had placed a good army in Michmash. In readiness, King Saul placed about six hundred men on the other side of the pass, at Gibeah. He was all set for war.

But Saul didn't attack. His finger was on the trigger, but he took no aim. The enemy sat comfortably in Israel, occupying and exploiting the good land. It was a phony war. Nobody did anything. The Philistines didn't need to do anything, but Israel should have done something.

> *They knew the Lord could save by the two of them. However, the Lord couldn't save at all, if everybody kept cool under the pomegranate trees.*

Now Jonathan was like David. They were soul mates with a similar, restless temperament of do or die. Jonathan became impatient just sitting there, fingering the blades of grass, one elbow on the ground. He thought of his father who "was sitting under a pomegranate tree," keeping cool.

Eventually, saying nothing to his father, Jonathan and his armor-bearer decided to take action themselves, just the two of them. The enemy was there. Why leave them unmolested? The Philistines would settle down in the land forever if something wasn't done.

TWO DARING DISCIPLES

Now the passage to the small Philistine garrison above them led through a narrow canyon which at one point passed between two sharp rocks. Jonathan not only would have to climb up, which gave the defenders an advantage over him, but he also would have to get through that narrow defensive position. One Philistine could hold off an army there, like Horatius did at the Tiber bridge. So Jonathan said to his shield bearer, "It may be that the LORD will work for us. For nothing restrains the LORD from saving by many or by few" (1 Sam. 14:6).

It was a venture of faith. They knew the Lord could save by the two of them. However, the Lord couldn't save at all, if everybody kept cool under the pomegranate trees. Such inaction would allow the occupying enemy to sit pretty forever. Some Israeli action was needed. It didn't matter to God whether it was done officially or by personal initiative.

So Jonathan and his friend decided on a test. They would come out of hiding and stand where the Philistines could see them. Then, if their enemies said, "Come up to us, and we will show you something" (1 Sam. 14:12), Jonathan and his armor-bearer would do just that. The Philistines never would have believed that they would attempt such a foolhardy escapade, two against twenty—an army close by—and the twenty soldiers in the commanding position above them.

Notice what Jonathan's test was. In it was an act of faith. He proposed to do something very courageous, and his "fleece" was that the Philistines would challenge him if he made himself conspicuous, something his enemies certainly would do. Some people put out "fleeces" which are absurd, and take guidance from conditions which are either too easy or too hard. These are those who usually get fleeced by the devil in the end.

The Philistines did see Jonathan, and said exactly what we might expect—"Come up to us." They, too, were not spoiling for battle at the time. They never believed the two young Israeli soldiers would attempt to go up. So they turned their backs and carried on, doing nothing in particular.

But, in faith, Jonathan and his armor-bearer did what was considered venturesome. The pair of them went up, creeping forward on hands and knees. They sprang an attack on the astonished garrison and caught them unprepared. Jonathan's faith gave him a sheer audacity which won the day.

Meanwhile, what was Saul doing? He was found talking to a priest of the Lord, probably seeking help and guidance, when it was obvious what his duty was. He hoped God would do something (1 Sam. 14:3). God *would* do something—as soon as somebody would believe Him and go into action.

And, in fact, God did do something—when Jonathan went into action. The daring attack came off. To begin with, the Lord honored their valor. Then He rose in His might and did His own thing. He brought about an earth tremor! (God is good at shaking the ground when people act in faith and also pray in faith. See Acts 4:31.)

The outcome was a panic attack. It spread throughout the enemy lines. The Philistine force became confused; rumors flew, soldiers scattered.

Jonathan's father, King Saul, heard the commotion. He found courage and led his men into the melee, giving chase. Even the prisoners whom the Philistines were holding took heart and turned on their captors. The Israeli people, who had hidden themselves among the rocks of Mount Ephraim, too frightened before to fight, now became bold and threw their weight into the rout of the enemy. Trapped, the Philistines' cause suffered a severe setback.

JUST AN ORDINARY DAY

Notice when this happened: "Now it happened one day." That means it was no special day. It was a day without divine leadings and revelations. The victory occurred because Jonathan made up his mind to fight. He made that day special himself. God's day coincided exactly with the day when Jonathan decided that Israel had hung around long enough.

The King had been waiting for something to happen, perhaps waiting to be pushed into action. He wanted a divine leading or hoped God would make the first move, which was why he talked to the priest. Jonathan couldn't hang around for eventualities and signs. He consulted no priest. His "fleece," testing God's will, was almost sure to put him into battle. No wonder Jonathan was a man after David's heart. And remember, David was a man after God's heart.

God has a thousand-year calendar with only one day on it. It is marked "TODAY." Jesus Himself challenged those who talked about waiting "four months and then comes the harvest," and said, "the fields are already white for harvest!" (John 4:35). The Prophet Haggai launched a blistering attack on people in

Jerusalem once when they said, "The time has not come, the time that the LORD'S house should be built" (Haggai 1:2). Their shameful priority was in building their own comfortable houses rather than a dwelling place for the glory of God.

THE INITIATIVE IS YOURS

Too often people say that the time isn't right. As if weather or circumstances could thwart the power of God! Revival isn't for when there is revival, but for when there isn't any sign of it. Revivals always begin when nothing is happening, when there are no signs of God's moving and when there is seemingly nothing encouraging on the horizon. Precisely

> *God has a thousand-year calendar with only one day on it. It is marked "TODAY."*

because things were bad all around, bold men and women of faith determined to change them. If we wait until the situation is better, we shall never go at all. In fact, what's the point then? Jonathan struck when a victory was impossible, and that is why he succeeded. God delighted to join in and prove His power.

We are all praying for a mighty revival to sweep America, Europe and the rest of the world. Pray on! But don't wait until it comes and Gospel preaching then becomes easy. Get on with what you can do now. You can win thousands for Christ while waiting for revival. And not only that; your action could be the very start of revival. It is true that revival is a sovereign act of God, as many believe. But it is equally true that revival can be caused. The early Christians certainly knew this, because Mark 16:20 declares:

And they went out and preached everywhere, the Lord working with them, and confirming the word with accompanying signs. Amen.

> *Anybody can believe God when God is already moving. Real faith acts when God doesn't seem to be moving! God loves the man and woman who gamble on His help!*

Those blessed believers didn't sit and wait for the Lord to go forth. Christians today say, "I will go when the Spirit moves me." No! The Gospel account declares, "And they went out . . ." In other words, *they* took the initiative, and the Lord gladly obliged! I am fully persuaded that God allows us to pull the trigger for mighty outpourings of His Holy Spirit.

By His grace, I have witnessed it numerous times! We need Holy Spirit initiative! Revival takes anointed men and women of God who exercise the audacity of faith!

When Jonathan and his armor-bearer went up by their own initiative, *and* on their hands and knees, to a private skirmish with the enemy, they brought about a far bigger victory than they thought possible. Is God waiting for you? Are you His Jonathan?

Anybody can believe God when God is already moving. Real faith acts when God doesn't seem to be moving! God loves the man and woman who gamble on His help! This is the formula for triumph, blessing and revival.

How many more people can you think of who did exactly that? Think of anybody who achieved new things for God, and you can put every one of them on this list. Every one was somebody who dared when nobody else thought it was the time. Every revival has started this way.

One minister longed for God's greater movings, to see the Lord heal the afflicted and work miracles. When he approached an older minister for counsel, he was told, "God will do those things when revival comes. So wait." The same atmosphere of unbelief permeated Nazareth when Jesus read from the Book of Isaiah concerning Himself and his miracle ministry. The unfriendly congregation put off, indefinitely, what God promised He would do. But Jesus declared, "*Today* this scripture is fulfilled in your hearing" (Luke 4:21, emphasis mine.)

Imagine this: Jesus teaching in the synagogue on the Sabbath. The cynics are there, watching Him. Another man is there, watching Him. This man has a withered hand. How much revival atmosphere could there be in this synagogue, with the critics waiting for a chance to accuse Jesus if He heals this man on the Sabbath? The conditions are hardly propitious. But Jesus heals the man—because *the time is ripe when the need is greatest* (Luke 6:6-11).

And the time, I am sure, is today. Who is God waiting for? Could it be you?

In conferences and church meetings I often say that you don't need anybody to lay hands on you. You don't need any more prophecies. All you need to do is to obey the Great Commission. Don't waste any more time. Go down to JCPenney and buy a suitcase!

What are you waiting for?

Chapter 16

NO BARGAINS WITH THE DEVIL

THE WHITE HORSE

From time to time, I'm invited to join a television panel to discuss religious issues. The participants generally meet just before going on the air. On one occasion, none of us knew each other, and we had to be introduced. There was a short time in which to chat with one another before the program began. Conversation got around to horse racing, as it was the time of the July Handicap. One of the men professed to be an atheist. He seemed to have the names of all the horses and jockeys at his fingertips. I couldn't say anything, as I had no knowledge of horse racing and betting. So, I sat quietly, occupying the time with silent prayer. I wanted the Lord to guide me in the discussion that soon would take place.

"Oh, Lord, when my turn comes," I prayed, "give me punching power!"

The others continued to discuss horses and gambling, and then, suddenly, something flashed through my spirit. It roused me, and I turned to the expert.

"Now I want to tell you something about horses," I said. The atheist turned to look at me with bemused interest. Baiting him, I said, "I have put all my money on the White Horse in the Book of Revelation."

Perhaps he thought I was an authority and had just been silent on the subject up to this point. The man looked baffled and repeated, "White Horse, in the Book of Revelation?"

This White Horse seemed to be the only horse that particular horse expert didn't know anything about.

"Well, tell me, who's the rider on the White Horse?," he asked. Of course, this question was exactly the one I had hoped to extract.

He wanted me to say who the jockey was! Well, it was exciting to tell him!

"In Revelation, Chapter 19, it says that the rider's name is 'Faithful and True, and the Word of God.' He is the Son of God, Jesus Christ, and," I added quickly, "Mister, I have not put just my money on Him. As a matter of fact, I have no money. I have put my life and my soul on Jesus Christ. He's the One I back with everything I've got, and I know I am going to win!" Atheism is intellectual vandalism and this atheist had to admit that he'd been gambling on all the wrong horses.

We know we are going to win because we have read about the Conqueror on the white horse in the back of the God's Book! The race starts for us with the finish—"a dead cert," in racing terms. For us, the end is a living certainty. It is the assurance of Jesus as the eternal and universal Winner. Knowledge like that is bound to have a tremendous effect upon our everyday lives.

THE UNCURSABLE WINNER

Do you know, with absolute assurance, that you have joined the winning side? Then you will not be harassed by fear. There is no way a believer can be crushed. He is uncursable. He has the Winner, God Himself, on his side. "If God is for us, who can be against us?" (Rom. 8:31).

Fear is forged in hell. It is issued by Satan as a standard weapon to all demons. They know the meaning of fear. It has a paralyzing force. Demons are full of fear themselves, like scorpions are full of poison. Fear is Satan's venom. He wants to sting us all, making us sick with fear. The devil will create a future for us packed with fears. But they are illusions—fears are mere phantoms. They only will take on substance if we accept them. We must exorcise these ghosts.

Fears are illusions—fears are mere phantoms. They only will take on substance if we accept them.

Fear is the first thing to get rid of. Satan will surround evangelism with a cloud of misgiving. Conquering dread is the blow against the enemy which neutralizes his primary attack. "No weapon formed against you shall prosper" (Isa. 54:17). We have our own weapon, the Word of God, the sword of the Spirit, that is the Word in the Hand of the Spirit (Eph. 6:17). Know the Word, learning from it that we are not at the mercy of the Evil One.

Do we, as believers, have to live in fear and dread of curses? Many people ask me how I "survive" all of the curses of African witchcraft. Don't they oppress me, they wonder? Don't those African witch doctor-curses get me down? But the Book of Proverbs tells us that undeserved curses will not alight (Prov. 26:2). We can look at an example, the story of Balak's plot to curse Israel (Numbers 22-24). Until now Israel had been undefeated on the battlefield. Balak, therefore, resorted to other means. He offered Balaam, the prophet, money to curse Israel. Balaam was willing. He loved money. He knew the Lord did not want to curse Israel, but He asked the Lord anyway, just in case, obviously to get the reward. He sought the Lord, hoping God would give him that kind of a prophecy.

Balak and Balaam clambered to the rocky peaks of the high places of Baal, building seven altars and offering seven bulls and rams in sacrifice as well. Perhaps some dark, occultic force might have obliged Balaam and Balak, blighting the progress of God's people.

But God does not deal in curses against His own people! Balaam and Balak persisted, however, trying hard from every angle. They found the attempt was futile as they surveyed the tents of Israel at the foot of the high hills. In the midst of the camp was the Tabernacle, with the glory cloud of God's Presence, the very banner of the Lord, constantly there. "He who keeps Israel shall neither slumber nor sleep" (Ps. 121:4). Israel was resting there early in the morning, safe beneath the outspread wings of Jehovah, which were invisible to Israel's enemies.

Balaam and Balak did their worst on the top of the mountain. Raging, they worked to cast a spell of misfortune over the Israelites. But the people of God slept on peacefully. Balaam opened his mouth to curse, but his words came forth as blessings instead. The tribes were there, all the time, still unaware and undisturbed. The Israelites were relaxing their heads on the pillow of His promises. They were safe under His divine protection.

The plotters' attempt to turn dark forces against Israel only succeeded in making them look ridiculous. I like the way the Bible concludes the episode. It has a touch of quiet mockery. "So Balaam rose and departed and returned to his place; Balak also went his way." That's all that happened!

Balaam, the prophet who lusted for profit, reluctantly gave the word of the Lord: "How shall I curse whom God has not cursed? And how shall I denounce whom the LORD has not denounced? The LORD his God is with him, and *the shout of a king is among them*" (Num. 23:8,21; emphasis mine).

FRIGHTENING SATAN

Fear plays into the hands of the devil. He can do no real damage, except to make us fear that he can. The devil is a con artist. Balaam was forced to speak the truth. He wound up showing us that God's people are not for cursing. We are immune. We are redeemed, as was Israel. What was true of God's redeemed people then, is true of the redeemed today. What glorious freedom from fear we enjoy!

Fear hears the hoarse shout of Goliath, but faith hears the shout of the King of kings. Hallelujah! The Lion of Judah has roared, and who can but prophesy (Amos 3:8)?

"There is no sorcery against Jacob, nor any divination against Israel. It now must be said of Jacob and of Israel, 'Oh, what God has done!'" (Num. 23:23). Incidentally, this verse reminds me of the many times that witch doctors and wizards attempted to curse our Gospel campaigns. Many times the proclamation of a simple but anointed, "Hallelujah!" from the platform has broken the yoke of oppression and sent witches wheezing and choking for breath! Their attempts to curse us and call up demons have been foiled by God's wall of fire and warrior angels. Truly, "The angel of the LORD encamps all around those who fear Him" (Psalm 34:7).

The howling winds of death had been heard across Egypt not long before. Yet, no Israeli home knew its cold breath. The blood of the lamb of the Passover marked every household. Jehovah, on hovering wings, protected them from the avenging angel. Every child of God today is covered and marked by the Blood of Jesus. Each one of us is beyond the reach of the powers of hell, of witches, of spells, of curses, of demons or of all the devil's minions. The principalities

Fear plays into the hands of the devil. He can do no real damage, except to make us fear that he can. The devil is a con artist.

and powers in heavenly places cannot touch us while we rest beneath the banner of the precious Blood of the Savior, our Passover Lamb. His protection surrounding us is impenetrable and invulnerable.

The man who fears is the devil's ally—whether he likes it or not. Fear is an infection, a sickness. It can spread among Christians. I am sure that the reason why God prohibited the children of Israel from talking while marching around the walls of Jericho was because they would have spread doubt and fear among themselves, (Josh. 6:10). The devil does not fear the man who fears. He knows that person is harmless. *But Satan trembles when we do not fear.*

Hundreds of years after Balak's encounter with Israel, Nehemiah was fearlessly restoring Jerusalem. Some urged him to hide from the threats of his enemies. I like his reply: "Should such a man as I flee? And who is there such as I who would go into the temple to save his life? I will not go in!" (Neh. 6:11). Are the people of God, the Blood-bought sons and daughters of the Kingdom, to give way to bluster and threats? God's people are not given "a spirit of fear, but of power and of love and of a sound mind" (2 Tim. 1:7). Should such a people as we are, flee? Never!

Far from fearing, we can rejoice. "Behold, I give you the authority to trample on serpents and scorpions, and over all the power of the enemy, and nothing shall by any means hurt you" (Luke 10:19). Christians are not the hunted, but the hunters; not the attacked, but the attackers. We are not besieged. We do not have our backs to the wall. Far from it! We are God's storm troops, sent to release the hostages of hell. We are the invading forces of the Lord!

Again and again, Jesus said, "Fear not!" But that was not all. He was the supreme Psychologist. Notice what He said: "Do not be afraid, only believe" (Luke 8:50). It was always more than just, "Don't be afraid," or "Take courage, be brave." That alone would be useless advice. Fear is a force and it must be met by a superior force, which is faith.

Fear is the negative force. Its sign is a minus. Somebody once said to me, "Fear is the darkroom in which people develop their negatives." Only a positive force can cancel a negative one. That positive force is faith. So Jesus always said, "Do not be afraid; only believe." The opposite of fear is not courage, but faith.

"And this is the victory that has overcome the world—our faith" (1 John 5:4). Faith is a multipurpose weapon. It is not presumption or bravado—remember the sons of Sceva (Acts 19:12-16). A trembling saint makes a triumphant Satan, but faith frightens the foe. We are not called to tremble, but to exercise authority and to shake hell.

"Benaiah . . . wrested the spear out of the Egyptian's hand, and killed him with his own spear" (2 Sam. 23:21). So we will snatch fear from the hands of the enemy, use his own weapon, and make devils tremble.

> *Christians are not the hunted, but the hunters; not the attacked, but the attackers. We are God's storm troops, sent to release the hostages of hell. We are the invading forces of the Lord!*

PRINCE OF THE POWER OF THE AIR

I had an experience during one of our Gospel crusades in Africa, which gave me a revelation. We were to use our Big Tent in Green Valley, South Africa. With great anticipation, I counted the hours to the first meeting, until the tent manager phoned. They were ready to pitch the canvas tabernacle, which, at that time, would hold 10,000 people, African style.

"The ground is too soft." The manager said, "In wind and rain the anchors and masts will lose their grip, and the tent could collapse. Wet soil will not support it." His question then was should he go ahead and pitch it or not? My mind was working fast on this question. It would be a terrible thing if it all went wrong. I prayed to the Lord in my heart while I thought. Then wonderful, divine assurance flooded my mind.

"Go ahead," I replied. "In the Name of Jesus, it is not going to rain or storm." And so, on that instruction, the tent went up.

We had a wonderful start. Night after night the tent was packed with people hungry for God. Then one afternoon, while I was kneeling in prayer in my trailer-caravan parked near the tent, I looked up and saw a mighty thunderstorm filling the western sky and heading in our direction. Have you ever seen an African storm, which fills the air with water? The clouds, like masses of pitch black curly hair, were being tossed by the storm within them.

Faith frightens Satan!

"Here comes your catastrophe," something said to me. Then I heard the Voice of the Holy Spirit answering that fear, telling me what to do: "Go and rebuke the devil!"

I went out and walked aggressively in the direction of the imminent storm. Lifting my finger and pointing, I said, "Devil, I want to talk to you in the Name of Jesus. If you destroy this tent of mine, I am going to trust God for a tent three times this size!"

I looked, and at that moment, something incredible happened—the clouds parted. They began to make a detour away from, and around, the tent. The menace was over! The clouds and rain never reached us, and the tent stood firm for the rest of the Gospel campaign.

"How great is Our God!"

Then this wonderful truth hit me harder than any thunder-bolt which that storm could have hurled at us: Faith frightens Satan! My faith had scared off the devil. He probably had enough to worry about already, with this tent of ours, and faith for a bigger one shook him.

"Devils tremble" the Bible declares in James 2:19. When we arise with living faith and tackle the opposition in God's strength, our faith terrorizes the archterrorist, Satan. "Resist the devil and he will flee from you," the Word declares (James 4:7). The Bible also instructs us to resist Satan: "Resist him, steadfast in the faith" (1 Pet. 5:9). This is no mere untried hypothesis. John could testify, "I write to you, young men, because you have overcome the wicked one" (1 John 2:13). With faith in God, "the lame take the prey" (Isa. 33:23).

But that tent episode was not quite over, for something unsettling nagged at my heart. "What if the devil misunderstood my words?" I wondered. The thought kept coming back to me. So, I decided to make the issue clear.

When things are impossible, faith is the answer. Faith is not just for the possible—that is not faith at all. The mightiest resource in the universe is the Arm of God.

I spoke to the devil in the name of Jesus once more, telling him, "I make no bargains with you. Just because you withdrew the wind and the rain does not mean I made an agreement with you about not having a bigger tent. The bigger tent comes anyway."

We are not to negotiate with the devil—we are to cast him out. That is all the Word of God tells us. Keep repeating to yourself, over and over if you must—faith frightens Satan, faith frightens Satan, faith frightens Satan. This truth will change you from negative to positive. In Jesus, you are the victor, not the victim. Satan is the victim, because Jesus crushed the serpent's head.

THE FEARLESS CHRISTIAN

God's children can be bold. Let the Word tell you so. "By faith Moses, when he was born, was hidden three months by his parents, because they saw he was a beautiful child; and they were not afraid of the king's command" (Heb. 11:23). Just think of what that involved. The Egyptian state and Pharaoh, its head, had made it illegal to keep a male Hebrew baby. By law, such children were to be killed at birth.

Soldiers moved around to carry out this order. What terror and grief there must have been!

Then Moses was born. His parents looked upon this lovely son, and they knew they could not, and never would, allow him to be killed. They decided to defy the law and hide the baby. "By faith . . . they were not afraid." Officers of the law were around, and their footsteps were heard stopping at their very door, seeking the child's life! Who would not shake in their shoes if armed men were waiting, ordered to kill their baby? Yet, "they were not afraid." Why not? Were they unnatural, unfeeling? No, they were very good parents. There was just one reason why they did not quiver or panic—they had faith in God. True, the situation was impossible. Their faith looked naive and foolish. But the situation was exactly what God likes. He delights to do the impossible.

When things are impossible, faith is the answer. Faith is not just for the possible—that is not faith at all. The mightiest resource in the universe is the Arm of God. Some can only believe God when it is for something "reasonable," something which can be managed. But, as Paul wrote, "We . . . have no confidence in the flesh" (Phil. 3:3), that is, in our own schemes.

I love to illustrate faith in a big God with the delightful African story of the elephant and the ant. An elephant crossed a shaky bridge, and a tiny ant sat on the elephant, just behind the huge animal's ear. The bridge shook as they crossed, and when they were safely on the other side, the ant said to the elephant, "My word! *We* made that bridge swing all right, didn't *we*?"

This is the relationship we have with God when we rest on Him. *He* carries us (Isa. 46:4). *He* makes the bridge swing. *He* puts His weight behind us and on our side. *He* builds your home, your church, your business. The Lord leads you to success. In Him, we find the impossible possible. Hallelujah!

THE WATERSHED

Faith makes the difference. It is the most basic distinction between one person and another. The entire world stands on one side or the other of the line of faith. There are only two really different types of people—not rich and poor, not black and white, not learned and unlearned, not Jew and Greek, not male and female. None of these distinctions really exist in Christ. God sees only believer and unbeliever. "He who believes . . . will be saved; but he who does not believe will be condemned" (Mark 16:16).

Faith is the new order. Unbelief is the old and dying order. Faith is the dividing line which runs right through mankind. Having faith, or having no faith at all, are the alternatives for our approach to life.

Faith is the new order. Unbelief is the old and dying order. Faith is the dividing line which runs right through mankind. Having faith, or having no faith at all, are the alternatives for our approach to life.

Fear sees just what man sees. Faith sees what God sees— and acts upon it. Faith creates action, and people of action, like Caleb and Joshua. Unbelief keeps us tied down in a spiritual wilderness—like Israel was for so many years. Fear and doubt magnify the difficulties, making us think people cannot be won for Christ and that the world is too strong. Without faith, we fear failure and mockery. But faith says people can be won, and so the joy of expectation grips us instead. By faith we move from minimum to maximum.

THE MAN WHO LIVED TOMORROW

There were two mummification processes used widely in Egypt. Nearly all the dead were preserved to stay in Egypt. The mighty Pharaohs were entombed in massive mausoleums,

> *Hundreds of years before it happened, Joseph shouted with the armies of men who, yet to be born, would bring down the walls of Jericho.*

multiple coffins, and even under permanent pyramids. Those dead people were very dead. But one of them had no intention of having "R.I.P." on his grave in Egypt. The mummy of Joseph was for export—the only one that ever was. Joseph knew the promises of God and what the future would hold, and he was determined not to be left out of it. Joseph, who died at age 110, wouldn't even be found dead in Egypt. He was the man who lived tomorrow.

"By faith . . . Joseph gave instructions concerning his bones" (Heb. 11:22). He didn't want to lie quietly in the grave when the Red Sea and the River Jordan opened. His eye of faith saw the faithfulness of God fulfilling His Word, that Word which He had given to Abraham, Isaac and Jacob long before. In fact hundreds of years before it happened, Joseph shouted with the armies of men who, yet to be born, would bring down the walls of Jericho. Faith renews our youth. A man of faith, at the age of 110 years, is younger than a critical teenager. So many of our young are "old" and futureless. They are the defeated rabble whose song is that of the Beatles: "Yesterday, all my troubles seemed so far away . . . I believe in yesterday." Without God and without hope. Where are the men of Joseph's battalion today?

God would go into action one day, and Joseph determined not to be left out of it, dead or alive. Faith gives life to the dead. It gives life to the fearful! Faith mocks at that King of Terrors, Death, and terrifies he who has the power of death, even the devil. "O Death, where is your sting?" (1 Cor. 15:55). Because Jesus the Conqueror lives, we too shall live—as conquerors in this life and in the life to come!

Part V

In Practice

Chapter 17

THE TRAP

GOD BLESSES HIS OWN PLANS

God underwrites His own schemes. He will supply, but we must know what His supplies are for. Cash is for the Lord's business. All we need to know is what He plans to do. Find out what God is engaged in, and throw your lot in with Him. Join the firm! Then we are authorized to requisition by faith what we need from His vast stores. We can ask God to provide for what we are doing, as long as we are doing what He does.

What is God in the business of doing? He is foremost the Savior, the God of salvation. "I, even I, am the LORD, and besides Me there is no savior" (Isa. 43:11). Salvation is not just an evangelist's pet subject, it is the Lord's principle work. God specializes in salvation. As medicine to a doctor, as music to a musician, so is the work of salvation to God. Jesus came "to seek and to save that which was lost" (Luke 19:10), and to bring "many sons to glory" (Heb. 2:10).

> *Salvation is not just an evangelist's pet subject, it is the Lord's principle work. God specializes in salvation.*

We are invited to work with Him, not on our own. The Gospel is God's business from start to finish—His monopoly, if you like. We can't set up Gospel shops for our own brand. Jesus Christ is the Head of all the salvation work in the world. We can labor in company with Him, and it must be done at all costs. He will meet those costs.

A friend of mine said, "If God is not the engine, I don't even want to give a push." Then I added, "But if God is the

When was God "careful," calculating every penny? Was He frugal when He sent His Own Son? He stripped heaven of its wealth and parted with its greatest treasure, His Only Begotten.

engine, I don't mind being the back light."

Move with God, and nothing can stop you. Nothing can go wrong with His plans. They don't fail or derail. What God wants to live cannot and will not die.

In some cases, church projects are surviving only under intensive care. They have little to do with God's plans. His life is not in them. Switch off the life-support machine! If real life is there, the programs will not need heart-lung equipment. What God wants to die—let die, and do not give it artificial respiration. "Let the dead bury their own dead," was Jesus' profound and refreshing advice (Luke 9:60). Why maintain unproductive church machinery and expect God to meet the bills? He won't. The real business of the Church is winning people for Christ.

WRONGFULLY AND RIGHTFULLY CAREFUL

When it comes to evangelism I've heard misguided people say, "We must be careful with God's money," as if He were a bit short of cash. It might be a sincere argument, but it sounds suspiciously stingy. Why hoard God's money in the bank? A church may save an emergency fund in order to have something for a rainy day. But God will look after any necessity that crops up. Besides, the most specific and urgent of emergencies already has come—the need to save the dying world!

When was God "careful," calculating every penny? Was He "thrifty" when He made the trillions of stars and planets, where not a soul lives? Was He frugal when He sent His Own Son? He stripped heaven of its wealth and parted with its greatest treasure, His Only Begotten. He divested Himself of all He loved and all He had for the salvation of our souls. "He who did not spare His own Son, but delivered Him up for us all, how shall He not with Him also freely give us all things?" (Rom. 8:32). Come on! We have an extravagant God!

GOD'S MONEY PLAN

The Lord fills our pockets for soul-saving. When we empty them, there will be more. God's money plan is simple. "Give, and it will be given to you" (Luke 6:38). Give, then you will have more to give more. God spares neither Himself nor dollars to find lost men and women. A church can't afford to save money instead of saving souls.

Spend to save! But spend it on soul-winning projects. People will give to a live project, but not to a dead bank account. When the collection takes longer than the preaching, something is wrong. The evangelism report should come before the treasurer's report. But the truth is, evangelism does not appear on the agenda at all in thousands of church business sessions. The bank statement often produces more discussion than the conversion figures of the month. Nevertheless, the church that gives, prospers. Evangelism and support of missions are essential for the health of a church. That has been proven too often to be doubted.

> *Many give God credit, but few give Him the cash He needs "to seek and to save that which was lost."*

TENTS AND INTENTS

God guides, then provides. He leads, then feeds. That is His rule of faith. An illustration is found with Israel. In the wilderness, manna fell where the pillar of cloud and fire went—and there only. If Israel missed God's guiding pillar, they missed breakfast, lunch and dinner. There is always enough if we are in the spot where He tells us to be.

> *In the wilderness, manna fell where the pillar of cloud and fire went—and there only. If Israel missed God's guiding pillar, they missed breakfast, lunch and dinner.*

When we were building our 34,000-seat tent in Africa, we were in dire need of finances. The Lord had told me not to take a bank loan, and His instructions are holy to me. Ringing in my ears were the words, "The silver is mine, and the gold is mine" Haggai 2:8). Then one day, a very large sum arrived. In fact, it was just what we needed. I hardly could believe my eyes—not because my faith was small. It was because of who sent the gift. The donor was a lady who, in the past, had sent us a couple of dollars a month. Then, suddenly, she mailed this large gift!

I felt this was something I had to know about. I visited her to find out what had prompted her to donate this amount. What she told me was almost too exciting to put into words. She said that, in the middle of the night, she received a telephone call. A voice had given her specific instructions to send this particular amount of money to us.

"But," she insisted, "the call was not from a human being. It was an angel of the Lord who spoke to me. I know that, because the glory of the Lord filled my room. I knew that God had given me a clear instruction. So I did just what He told me."

Well, I thought, if God put an angel in charge of our finances, I need have no sleepless nights. I can sleep the sleep of the just and relax, as long as I am in partnership with Him.

WHOSE DONKEY IS IT ANYWAY?

Although the Lord told me not to take out a bank loan at that time, that does not mean bank loans are necessarily wrong. We should not condemn those who are led differently from ourselves. God provided manna from the skies, but He has other ways, also. Jesus Himself used different methods. Let us look at one of them. When Jesus prepared for His triumphal entry into Jerusalem, He needed an animal to ride upon. This is what happened:

> And it came to pass, when He drew near to Bethphage and Bethany, at the mountain called Olivet, that He sent two of His disciples, saying, "Go into the village opposite you, where as you enter you will find a colt tied, on which no one has ever sat. Loose it and bring it here. And if anyone asks you, 'Why are you loosing it?' thus you shall say to him, 'Because the Lord has need of it.'" (Luke 19:29-31)

Matthew's account tells us that Jesus also had a colt with the donkey. Jesus did not call a prayer meeting to pray for the acquisition of these animals. He took the initiative in this case: "Go into the village . . . loose it and bring it . . . the Lord has need of it." The Lord was the One who had created all the donkeys there were. Why did He have to ask for one? The unusual details in this account tell me

A church can't afford to save money instead of saving souls. Spend to save! But spend it on soul-winning projects.

that the Lord has needs. And He gives us the privilege of fulfilling them! "The Lord has need . . ."

His work has needs which you, I and all God's children can supply. It is God's wonderful arrangement to give us the joy of sharing with Him in what He does. This ought to make us happy. I imagine that later the owner of the donkey, after he understood, must have thanked the Lord all his life for this privilege. Even the little donkey had its day! He had helped Jesus a mile or two along His way to triumph.

I noticed that the man had "securely tightened" his donkey. It was his "capital," and he didn't want to lose it. The Lord told His disciples to "loose" it. Let's untie our donkeys for Jesus! Jesus always taught that we should not hold tightly to our money. Many give God credit, but few give Him the cash He needs "to seek and to save that which was lost." We should loose our donkeys now, or we may lose them in the end. As the writer said: "We lose what on ourselves we spend, we have as treasure without end, whatever Lord to Thee we lend, who givest all."

It is, of course, Biblical to take up offerings to do what God wants done. God loves a cheerful giver, because He is one Himself. Nobody can evangelize the world alone. We all have gifts to contribute: money, talents, time or ourselves. Only the total contribution of all of us can accomplish the task. Together is the only way it can be done. Not an idle hand, for the laborers are so few, and not an idle dollar, for the needs are so many.

THE MONEY TRAP

Money can be a booby trap for the unwary. We need pure hearts, pure motives and God's anointing upon our eyes to perceive the snares of the devil. I had just started to reach out to Africa when the Lord sent me an extraordinary qualifying test. A lady phoned with a fantastic financial offer for the ministry. I paid her a visit to discuss the details. Her home exuded an atmosphere of wealth and opulence.

"I have wanted to meet you," she greeted me cordially, "because I have watched you for some time."

She soon came to the point, and it was so wildly beyond my imagination that I could only stare in wide-eyed amazement. She said, "I want to finance your Gospel crusades in Africa."

I almost forgot to breathe! On the table was a file, which she pushed across to me. It contained documents setting out her financial assets. I read as if I had discovered the El Dorado.

"You can see what I own," she said. "Iron ore deposits, a diamond mine, et cetera." It was like meeting Rockefeller.

"Now," she explained, "I want to form a trust and give half my assets to the work of God. Would you like to join the trustees? All this money is to be used in the service of the Lord. Will you accept it?"

Surely God was behind such liberality? Yet I heard no echo of pleasure from heaven. There was no witness in my spirit. Instead, I felt a strange caution, though I tried to hide my lack of enthusiasm. All I could say was, "Thank you! But this is a great responsibility. Could I pray about it before committing myself?"

My wife Anni was experiencing the same reaction. No excitement, but instead a feeling more like anxiety. We knew we must get down before the Lord about this and ask for His guidance.

"Lord, if this is a trap of the devil, we'll have nothing to do with it," we prayed.

Occupied with our crusades, weeks passed. We could not bring ourselves to say either yes or no to the seemingly fantastic offer. Meanwhile, one night I had a fearful nightmare which I could not forget. I dreamed that I stood on a river bank at dusk. The water was low, leaving only puddles and mud. A small man passed me and walked down the embankment. He beckoned me, and I followed. When I was in the middle, suddenly, with an awful roar, a huge hippopotamus rose in front of me. There are two species, and this was the biggest one! I backed away from its engulfing jaws, but there was another of the monsters looming behind me. Still others arose from the mud, and I was surrounded on all sides by harrying hippos! In peril and despair, I cried out, "Jesus, help me!"

While that nightmare was still fresh in my mind, the lady contacted me again and pressed me to make a decision. We agreed to another visit, and she welcomed us again with a smile. She said, "Before we go into the house, let me show you around here." So we went with her. After a while we come to where her grounds ended at a river.

All at once, a shock went through me, as if I had been struck by lightning. That river! There it was—the same as in my nightmare. The river was identical, and now I was not dreaming. There was peril lurking here—that was what the dream meant. God had shown me. I felt the Lord near me, and I was sure my answer was coming. So I asked if we could go into the house and have prayer together.

As soon as we knelt, I heard the Voice of the Lord not once, but three times. "My son, have nothing to do with this." I said to the wealthy lady, "Please allow me to decline your great generosity. Give your millions to someone else. God does not want me to have this money." At that moment, a weight lifted from my spirit. Why? It seemed so strange. But God did something else at that moment. By His Spirit, He showed me my true assets, the promises in His Word. "My God shall supply all your need according to His riches in glory" (Phil. 4:19).

I realized that I could exhaust the millions the lady was offering, and when they were finished, my ministry could be finished also, because I would not have continued to learn to rely on the Lord.

PROMISSORY NOTE

This trust fund was not to be my source of supply. God had His own trust. I must do the trusting. In fact, God had planned an even greater source than this lady's fund. I had the divine promissory note—His riches, inexhaustible, backed by His own guarantees. El Shaddai—that name means All Sufficient, not penny-pinching. I was more blessed by these precious promises than by all the gold and diamonds in the world.

The Lord instructed me by saying, "The baskets of the disciples started filling only after the multitudes had all eaten. Keep on feeding the multitudes with My Word and I will see to filling up the baskets."

Somehow, I felt as if I had just passed a very difficult test and had progressed in the school of the Holy Spirit. I had learned that, for as long as I would continue to preach the Gospel, regardless of how much it cost, the Lord would see that the bills were met. What God orders to be done, He pays for, and, if necessary, He will move heaven and earth to do it.

GIVING ROYALLY

I've quoted Philippians 4:19, "My God shall supply all your need according to His riches in glory by Christ Jesus." The phrase "according to" (from the Greek word "kata") means "by the standard of." That is, by the standard of His riches, not the standard of our poverty. He fills our empty sack, but does not measure it first. He gives as a king does, "running over," not as someone of modest means would be able to give. Don't ask, "Lord, can you manage to send me $9.50, please? I think You can get by with that. I hope You don't mind." Tell Him your need! Let Him supply. He has a big Hand.

His guests don't sit down to dry crusts; He is the Producer of all the fruit of the field. Giving does not impoverish Him. He always gives. The *"indescribable gift"* of His Beloved Son is God's style of generosity. His scale is worthy of His greatness.

My visit to that diamond farm hammered something else into my mind. "Never compromise because of money." Don't sell your soul for a plate of red stew.

What God orders to be done, He pays for, and, if necessary, He will move Heaven and earth to do it.

Later on, when I felt the Lord tell me to order the first big Gospel tent, I stood there and said, "Lord, I am a poor missionary. Look, my pockets are empty!" The Lord replied, "Don't plan with what is in your pocket, but with what is in Mine." I looked into His pockets and saw that they were full. I said, "Lord, if You allow me to plan with what is in Your pockets, then I will plan like a millionaire." I then began to do so, literally. I've found that God is as rich as He said, and as good. To Him be glory! While doing His perfect will we can ask God, not just for a loaf of bread, but for the whole bakery! His servants don't have to scramble for a piece of the pie, or fight over the crumbs. Look in God's shop window—it is full of delicious and satisfying baked goods.

TWELVE BASKETS FULL

Tests? Trials of faith? They will come. They come to me, anyway. I remember sitting on the side of my bed in Malawi. I had a three dollar per day room in a Baptist hostel. But I had to sit down because a shock had just hit me. An urgent phone call from my office in Frankfurt, Germany had brought me news I couldn't take in. We were hundreds of thousands of dollars in the red! How could that be?

At the beginning of that year, the Lord had assured me it would be "a year of twelve full baskets, a basket for each month." I couldn't see how we could be in debt.

"Lord," I said, "Why? You said there would be full baskets. But they are all empty. How can that be?"

In such moments, the Lord opens our eyes. He instructed me by saying, "The baskets of the disciples started filling only after the multitudes had all eaten. Keep on feeding the multitudes with My Word and I will see to filling up the baskets." I was amazed. The divine wisdom made sense. I said, "Lord, I will do what You say, and I know You will do what You say."

But—hundreds of thousands of dollars! It seemed beyond reason. Yes, but God reasons differently. The baskets stayed empty for 24 hours, and then came the news that God had filled them again. The year ended without debt. We had just kept on feeding the multitudes with the Word of God, and the Lord had just kept handing the supplies to us.

When we are breaking the Bread of Life to the spiritually starving, God cannot let us down. That year, we saw 1,500,000 precious people respond to the call of God to be saved in our African crusades alone.

NOT A SANDAL STRAP THE WORLD'S WAY

In Genesis, there is a familiar story about Abraham and Lot. Lot, the nephew of Abraham, had been carried off by Chedorlaomer after a battle against five kings. One of the defeated kings was the King of Sodom. Abraham, with some confederates, went to the rescue and recovered everything Chedorlaomer had taken, including the captives.

The King of Sodom then started to tell Abraham what to do with the spoils, "Give me the persons, and take the goods for yourself" (Gen. 14:21). That was the whole idea in those days.

One country pillaged another, like parasites. But now the King of Sodom was in for a surprise. Abraham replied:

> "I have raised my hand to the LORD, God Most High, the Possessor of heaven and earth, that I will take nothing, from a thread to a sandal strap, and that I will not take anything that is yours, lest you should say, 'I have made Abram rich.'" (Gen. 14:22-23)

That king had come up against something new in the world. Abraham was a man with a new way of life—faith in God. He was one of God's VIPs. In his hands, he held a blue print for "a city, . . . whose builder and maker is God" (Heb. 11:10).

The way of the world was finished for Abraham. His life had been handed over to God, and he was the Lord's personal responsibility. Abraham had the Word and the promise of the Almighty God.

Then God said, "Abram . . . I am your exceeding great reward" (Gen. 15:1). Later, we discover that "the LORD had blessed Abraham in all things" (Gen. 24:1). *All things!* That is Bible language, not the world's.

> How shall He not with Him also freely give us all things? (Rom. 8:32)

> "For your heavenly Father knows that you need all these things." (Matt 6:32)

> "And all these things shall be added to you." (Matt. 6:33)

> His divine power has given to us all things. (2 Peter 1:3)

> For all things are yours. (1 Cor. 3:21)

That is the Abraham way. Be a child of Abraham! Trust God to the uttermost.

He cannot and will not fail.

Chapter 18

HISTORY ON THE ROPE

The eyes of Jesus seem to look at me from behind the lines of print in my Bible, as from behind a lattice. Everywhere I trace Him I cannot interpret incorrectly if His face becomes clearer. I read the following passage as if I were there. The story merged with a vaster scene, which I hope you will see as vividly and movingly as the vision appeared to me.

> David was then in the stronghold, and the garrison of the Philistines was then in Bethlehem. And David said with longing, "Oh, that someone would give me a drink of the water from the well of Bethlehem, which is by the gate!" So the three mighty men broke through the camp of the Philistines, drew water from the well of Bethlehem that was by the gate, and took it and brought it to David. Nevertheless he would not drink it, but poured it out to the LORD. And he said, "Far be it from me, O LORD, that I should do this! Is this not the blood of the men who went in jeopardy of their lives?" Therefore he would not drink it. These things were done by the three mighty men. (2 Sam. 23:14-17)

THE SIGH AND THE CRY FOR WATER

David was thirsty and sighed, "Oh, that someone would give me a drink of the water from the well of Bethlehem, which is by the gate!" That particular well, however, was situated behind enemy lines. The Philistines held it. Standing near, within earshot as David spoke his inner wish out aloud, were several of his best warriors. To them, David's wish was their command. Three of them looked at one another, nodded to each other and formed an instant partnership. Without a further word, they set out together on a special mission to fulfill David's desire.

They knew the dangers. They might have to pay for a cup of water for David with their life blood. But such considerations gave them not a moment's hesitation. Protest and complaint were out of the question. What David wanted must be supplied, even though he would never have sent them himself. David was their lord. They knew his mind, and that was enough. Risks were their common duty. Loyalty does not wait for orders. Hesitation would suggest that they were reluctant to please their leader.

The wish of David for a drink brings to mind the far more important words of Jesus as He hung on the Cross. He also cried, "I thirst!" (John 19:28). His thirst was, no doubt, physical, but it reached beyond the physical. His great thirst was for the salvation of men and women.

It was that thirst which brought Him to earth and to the cross. His physical thirst was only the result of His infinite desire for the souls of His creatures.

That cry from the Cross of *"I thirst!"* rings in our ears forever, having a far deeper meaning than David's, "I thirst." How many recognize that fact? Have we ears to hear, or do we conveniently not catch the true import of those two words? Do we give serious attention to that cry from the Cross, allowing it to move our hearts and our lives to action? Is that cry being heard now by anyone?

For a wish little more than a whim, David's men set out to please him. They could have brought water from a safer place, perhaps better water, in fact, but that would not have satisfied their sense of utter devotion to their lord. For David, they did not count their lives dear to them.

I am challenged. How many of us would be as ready to act similarly for our Lord Jesus? We know His desire—the salvation of souls—but do we need urgings and commands before we acknowledge it? Isn't a knowledge of His thirst our immediate obligation to act? What could be a louder call than the desires of the Son of God? Even if it should mean putting our lives at risk, remember that men risked their lives for a mere cup of water for David. And how often is danger involved, anyhow, in fulfilling the desire of the Son of God?

THE WELL OF BETHLEHEM

Now the well of Bethlehem was surrounded by enemy troops. But David's three warriors took their swords, along with their water vessel, and began their exploit. The well was sunk very deep into the ground, which increased the danger involved. The precious waters were deep down, yet this was the water David longed for. Somebody had to go down and bring it up.

> *Multitudes who are in the depths of darkness have to be reached. Whole nations are in spiritual graves. Somebody has to go down and do the job.*

What a vivid picture this is of evangelism! Multitudes who are in the depths of darkness have to be reached. They must be brought up to the light—coming from death to life. Whole nations are in spiritual graves. Somebody has to go down and do the job. The well of Bethlehem was in Philistine hands, just as precious souls are caught in Satan's grip. This meant that the warriors first had to break through enemy lines. There was a skirmish and then a breakthrough. Those three men were driven and strengthened by their determination to bring their commander-in-chief something they merely had overheard was his wish.

HOLDING THE ROPE

A well normally has some mechanical means with which to heave up the water. But, in order to connect with our New Testament picture, let us imagine that there were no such means. Those three men were faced with a very hard task

World outreach today needs, and always has needed, those who are willing to go down and those who are willing to hold the rope! That rope is a lifeline.

when they arrived at the well. The warriors had to organize themselves and decide who should go down into the well. It meant that while one slid down on a rope, the others would have to hold him while watching to ward off the enemy.

This is certainly the method of world evangelism. Teamwork is absolutely essential. World outreach today needs, and always has needed, those who are willing to go down and those who are willing to hold the rope! That rope is the support line of the ones who have gone down, and those who hold it are just as important as those who go down. The supporters dare not slacken their hold on the rope until the man with the water is all the way up. That rope is a lifeline. Not even a "coffee break" is possible for those who are holding it! Any relaxation of grip, and the man depending on that rope is lost. Precious men and women who go out at the desire of Jesus, in order to bring Him the waters He longs for, are in exactly the same position. Without the rope holders (the supporters), tragedy would occur.

KINGDOM LOGISTICS

It is a most serious matter when anyone today says that we should cut back on our commitment to world evangelism. Due to pressing domestic economic problems, world need is pushed aside for local need. My deep conviction is this—we cannot afford to slacken our hands on the rope of support for those who have risked so much for the task. Too much depends on their efforts. The evangelists and missionaries themselves depend on that lifeline, and, even more importantly, the whole Gospel project of Christ (which is His water), also must reach our Heavenly David!

These are Kingdom of God logistics. I praise God for the men and women who back us with prayer and intercession, thus keeping the tension on the rope. I certainly remember many days when I have been fishing deep in the darkness of those wells or pits across the world, and have felt the presence of the hosts of hell. Yet, every time, I knew that there were faithful prayer partners who held my rope and stood with me night and day. Thank God for these rope holders!

Eventually, David's warrior on the end of the rope was pulled out of the well. In his hands he held the container with the precious water. All three men rejoiced and immediately began their journey back home. I can imagine that the two flanked the one carrying the precious water on his left and right sides. How carefully the warrior carried the vessel! Under no circumstances did he want to lose one drop of what he had gone to fetch. The men on each side held their swords in their hands, and they opened the way for the middle man. It was perfect teamwork.

> *The Kingdom of God also depends upon the union of Holy Spirit anointed ministries. Evangelism and missions require the sum total of all contributory effort.*

The Kingdom of God also depends upon the union of Holy Spirit anointed ministries. Evangelism and missions require the sum total of all contributory effort. "Like a mighty army moves the church of God," we sing, but this needs to be a reality if we are to fulfill The Great Commission.

INCONSPICUOUS HEROES OF HEAVEN

The warriors finally arrived at the tent of David, their lord, with the water and their blood-stained swords. But then, amazingly, he refused to drink the water! He realized that they

Suppose the Apostle Paul had not escaped those seeking to assassinate him, or that his rope holders had let his basket crash to his death! He was the man who brought Christianity to Europe. If they had known that the destinies of nations dangled on the end of that one little rope, how much tighter might they have gripped it!

had risked their very blood to bring it to him. When David honored this deed, he ranked all three of these men as *heroes*! Some might have honored only the one who had gone down into the pit, but not so with David. All three warriors had a vital part in bringing about this victory.

One day, we will kneel before our Heavenly David. All God's children will be there—those who went down into the pits, as well as those who faithfully held the ropes. I am sure that we will witness a great many surprises. Those who had been so inconspicuous will, all of a sudden, be *heroes* in the Kingdom of God. Their reward will be great. The Lord will not say, "much done" but, "well done, good and faithful servant" (Matt. 25:21).

A JANITOR A HERO?

A pastor in Germany told me of one old lady in his church whose job it was to clean the church building. She came to him and said that she had had a wonderful dream. She dreamed she stood before the gate of eternity. Many people were lined up, and she joined them. Then she realized that all the people in front of her held sheaves in their arms, while she presented only a few grains of wheat. She felt very uncomfortable and let others, who came behind her, move in front. Then, suddenly, the gate opened, and her name was called. It was the Lord. Trembling, she stepped forward with those pitiful grains in her hand. But the Lord spoke comforting words to her: "You have been faithful over few, I will put you over much." Then she woke up. The pastor told me that, exactly a week after this dream, the lady died. I was deeply touched. Holding the rope is not always glamorous, but it surely is worthwhile. As Esther Kerr Rusthoi writes: "It will be worth it all, when we see Jesus."

Let us not relax! Keep on bringing to Jesus the "water" that will quench His thirst. He thirsts—He desires to have with Him in His salvation kingdom, men and women, boys and girls. He longs for them to hear and accept the Gospel. That is what evangelism is all about.

Although the pit is deeper and darker than ever, we will be more productive than ever *if* we work hand in hand. God is faithful. If we are to fulfill the Word of the Lord, we must be ready to go down to the lost, or else be ready to keep firmly grasping the supporting rope.

HISTORY ON THE END OF A ROPE

The men from David's army were not the only men who held on to ropes. We remember that Jeremiah, the great prophet, was pulled from a pit, and that Joseph's rescue eventually prevented famine in that ancient world. There were men who, when his life was at stake, let Paul down over the wall of Damascus in a basket. All these helpers only grasped ropes, yet they all held future history in their hands.

Suppose Joseph had been abandoned in the pit. What would have happened to Egypt and to Jacob's family, as well as to a future son of Jacob, our Lord Jesus? It is quite awful to think this thought through to the end.

Suppose Jeremiah had not been rescued, and that his work had perished with him in that horrible pit. Would we have had his prophecies, and would Israel, through these long centuries, have drawn the comfort and hope which was theirs through his words? But somebody held the rope, and Jeremiah was rescued.

Suppose the Apostle Paul had not escaped those seeking to assassinate him, or that his rope holders had let his basket crash to his death! He was the man who brought Christianity to Europe. If they had known that the destinies of nations dangled on the end of that one little rope, how much tighter might they have gripped it! But they held on strongly enough, and we are eternally blessed, thanks to them.

I am convinced in my heart that those who are Rope Holders in world evangelism today are making history for time and eternity. Can you feel the pull? Do you hear the multitudes calling upon the Name of the Lord for salvation? Do you see that massive exodus from the kingdom of darkness into the marvelous light of God? These precious souls saved are the future citizens of the New Jerusalem. Today we cannot afford to reduce global efforts to bring the Gospel of salvation to the nations. We dare not do less, but must do more. Too much is at stake. The eternity of millions depends on what we do *today*.

At the same time, I would like to thank all those faithful men and women who have been and are our rope holders, whether they hold the ropes of intercession or the ropes of financial support. Some glorious morning, when we kneel at the feet of Jesus, they will receive their great reward.

Our support is for whom? We cannot tell, but somebody, somewhere, is holding a new future in their hands for many—possibly for the whole world.

To save a world, hold the rope—that is all that you may be asked to do, but it is critically vital. To lose a world, don't bother to lend a hand—that is all you have to do.

Chapter 19

INTEGRITY: THE SATANIC TARGET

THE BEGINNING IS IN THE END

When I was a young minister, I attended a pastor's conference where there was great blessing. The power of God fell and we went down on our knees before the Lord. An old servant of God in his nineties knelt next to me, and he prayed with such earnestness that I couldn't help but hear and watch him.

This is what he prayed: "Lord, forgive me where I have allowed those things in my life and ministry that were not clean . . ."

His prayer moved me so deeply that I followed with my own: "Lord, please help me. May I never allow anything unclean in my life and ministry. Help me so that, when I am old, I need not pray a prayer like my precious brother has just prayed."

Keep your mind set in the beginning on what matters in the end!

If you desire to be a minister of the Lord, then hear the Word of the Lord: keep your mind set in the beginning on what matters in the end! You are responsible for the integrity of Christ before the world. Walk circumspectly.

SATANIC STRATEGY

Christians who are at the forefront are prime targets for Satan—and for attacks of the media, as well. Neither the devil nor the press are shining examples of accuracy or mercy. Weakness in response to Satanic hatred has caused stumbling by some of God's servants lately. The tragedies of sin have been welcome copy to the scandal sheets, which covered the indiscretions with full orchestration and glee. David wrote a poetic lament mourning the death of his mortal foe, King Saul.

But modern writers are smaller men, of less nobility and civilization. They often maximize the damage to the Kingdom of God.

> *The enemy may lull us into a sense of false immunity.*
> *Mild temptations, resisted, help deceive us about our moral strength.*
> *Then Satan turns his big guns upon our unguarded flanks—just where we thought we were so strong!*
> *Guard your "strong" points!*

I want to put you on your guard. The devil is very patient. He is unrelenting and merciless. Hell will brood and plot for years, engineering indescribably subtle and custom-made circumstances to bring about your downfall. He will devise traps right on your very doorstep, and you will need anointed eyes to be able to detect them.

Demon powers will try every devious means to encompass and destroy a believer's testimony. The devil is a full-time professional opponent. Christ repulsed him, so, biding his time, the devil attacked the disciples (Luke 22:31). First, Judas betrayed Jesus; then Peter denied Him with oaths and curses; and the rest forsook the Lord and fled, right at His crisis hour (Matt. 26:56). Incredible!

The enemy may lull us into a sense of false immunity. Often mild temptations, resisted, help deceive us about our moral strength. Then Satan turns his big guns upon our unguarded flanks—just where we thought we were so strong! Guard your "strong" points! We can despise those who fall, which is a way of drawing attention to our own superior holiness. Remember— better men have fallen. Never underestimate satanic subtlety. Only saving grace preserves our feet from slipping.

If you consider spiritual warfare, remember that its main battleground is in your own heart and mind, not up in the skies somewhere. "Keep your heart with all diligence, for out of it spring the issues of life" (Prov. 4:23). Before you go into combat daily, "Watch and pray, lest you enter into temptation" (Matt. 26:41).

Right at the start make a covenant with God to live a holy life. Remember that determination alone will not do it. Success, in and of yourself, is not guaranteed, even with a contract written with a pen dipped in blood. The arm of flesh will fail. Here is a better way.

THE FIRST KEY—
A CELESTIAL EXAMPLE OF PERFECT SERVICE

He is able to keep you from stumbling (Jude 24). But how? That is the frequent question. How can we serve perfectly? A key is found in Isaiah 6:1-3:

> "In the year that King Uzziah died, I saw the LORD sitting on a throne, high and lifted up, and the train of His robe filled the temple. Above it stood seraphim; each one had six wings: with two he covered his face, with two he covered his feet, and with two he flew. And one cried to another and said: "Holy, holy, holy is the LORD of hosts; the whole earth is full of His glory!"

The seraphim are throne angels of the Most High. Nothing sullied would be allowed so close to God and the seat of all power in heaven, on earth, and under the earth. Isaiah saw these celestial intelligences serving the Lord in the holiest place of all, the atmosphere of God's immediate presence. Somewhere here is a challenge to purity, along with the way to achieve it. These creatures are our models.

A notable feature about the seraphim is that they each had six wings:

Two wings covered their faces, which speaks of humility.
Two wings covered their feet, which speaks of purity.

With two wings, they flew, which speaks of worship and praise.

HUMILITY

First, why did these mighty beings cover their glorious and beautiful faces and prevent the young prophet Isaiah from seeing them? Because they would not prevent him from seeing the Lord. The seraphim would not "upstage" the Lord and distract Isaiah's gaze from the Throne.

Notice also, that though they were holy creatures themselves, they only spoke of the holiness of the Lord and of His glory. Humility is part of holiness.

We learn the same lesson when Jesus was transfigured on the mountain before his disciples Peter, James and John (Matt. 17:1-8). In those glorious moments, Moses and Elijah also appeared. We read, that presently the disciples saw Jesus only—the two prophets having withdrawn from view. The Father's interest was similar. He did not talk to the disciples about the two great prophets of Israel. Rather, He said, "This is My beloved Son, in whom I am well pleased. Hear Him!"

Jesus Christ, the Son of God, is the center, the focus for all. Every miracle comes from Him. What room is there for human pride? Heavenly seraphs, princes of glory burning like flames, hid their own attractions. Moses and Elijah in their glory, giants among redeemed immortals, retired into the background. How much more should we, fragile and fading earth folk, decrease so that He might increase?

Herein lies a spiritual risk for all servants of the Lord. Are we working for recognition or to make a name for ourselves? Do we just want "big meetings" to use the tens or hundreds of thousands of people for a backdrop to highlight our own importance or our imagined greatness? The Light from the Cross is not the limelight for any preacher! Jesus Christ did not die to give us a career, but to save the lost!

Aim to dazzle and you dim God's glory. Preach for personal admiration and people who come to see God will only see the preacher. What did the great evangelist and apostle, Paul, say? "For if I preach the gospel, I have nothing to boast of, for necessity is laid upon me; yes, woe is me if I do not preach the gospel!" (1 Cor. 9:16).

> *The Light from the Cross is not the limelight for any preacher! Jesus Christ did not die to give us a career, but to save the lost!*

The character of John the Baptist should lead us to a sobering view of ourselves. Some wondered if he was the Messiah himself. Even Christ said John was the greatest born of women. When more people began to turn to Christ than were following John's ministry, John's followers were jealous. But John wasn't. He told them that Jesus must increase, and he declared, "I must decrease." When half the nation came, he pointed away from himself to Jesus. At the river he cried, "Behold! the Lamb of God." Every single thing that John said about himself was a declaration of his own lowliness. Greatness begins and ends with humility. That is what it means to cover one's face.

The Lord is a jealous God. He declares in no uncertain terms, "My glory I will not give to another" (Isa. 42:8). To be proud in the presence of the King of kings is to touch the very Ark of God, a sin for which Uzzah died (2 Sam. 6:6-7). Herod puffed up like a bull frog when a crowd shouted that he was a god. He was quickly struck down. "Because he did not give glory to God," he was "eaten by worms," a terrible disease known by doctors today (Acts 12:21-23).

Those privileged to exercise the gifts of the Spirit must be especially careful. Show-offs will be shown up. Spiritual gifts are not Oscars for display, won as trophies of performance. Don't decorate yourself ostentatiously with God's power tools. Don't design tiaras, necklaces and rings from the spiritual gifts for your own adornment.

The sentry of your heart's door is called "Humility." Dismiss that guardian and the unprotected gate is soon battered in, with the enemy taking over.

PURITY IS NEXT TO PROBITY

The second pair of wings covered the seraphim's feet. This action signified purity. The cleanest man makes contact with the ground as he walks. There was no dust near the Throne, of course, but the seraphim's act was symbolic. It signaled the need to walk in holiness before the Lord.

Jesus made a special point of this. He stooped to wash the feet of the disciples. Such cleansing was needed. He said, "He who is bathed needs only to wash his feet, but is completely clean" (John 13:10).

> *The sentry of your heart's door is called "Humility." Dismiss that guardian and the unprotected gate is soon battered in, with the enemy taking over.*

First, we must watch where we walk. Make no provision for the works of the flesh, Paul suggested in Romans 13:14. Don't pray, "And do not lead us into temptation," and then land yourself in it. Unclean feet are the symbol of a careless walk. "Be clean, you who bear the vessels of the LORD" (Isa. 52:11).

Such advice, we all know, is more easily given than taken. The modern media pour moral pollution into the atmosphere, like chimneys belching soot. We need a gas mask not to breathe in the soul diseases of a materialistic age with its accompanying unbelief. Diligence is one thing, certainly, but we need other help. What is it?

Our best safeguard is using the Word to wash our minds constantly. Our thought life, conditioned by the Word of God and the covering of the Blood of Jesus, is impregnable. "Gird up the loins of your mind" (1 Peter 1:13), by the daily reading of the Word. It is an immunization injection against all spiritual infections. "Your word I have hidden in my heart, that I might not sin against You!" (Ps. 119:11). Scientists have produced a polish for cars which simply rejects dirt. Long before such scientific experiments, believers found that the power of the Word repulses sin.

How can we do as Scripture says—"whatever things are lovely . . . meditate on these things" (Phil. 4:8)? To begin with, the Bible gives us things that are lovely to think on, as

> *Our best safeguard is using the Word to wash our minds constantly. Our thought life, conditioned by the Word of God and the covering of the Blood of Jesus, is impregnable.*

well as fortifying to our desires and motives. Pray also, "do not lead us into temptation," and "watch and pray." *And never presume you do not need to do so.*

Do you want glorious liberty in the Spirit? Then stand before men with an open countenance on any platform, your motives transparent, with no shame to conceal. This is an experience and a state of being that is worth everything. Better still, you can have confidence as you stand before God. "Beloved, if our heart does not condemn us, we have confidence toward God" (1 John 3:21). *But if your heart condemns you even slightly, your witness for the Lord will be weakened.*

We often sermonize about Esau selling his birthright for a bowl of stew, but a whole generation of Israel lost the Promised Land and died in the wilderness because they moaned for Egypt's cucumbers (Num 11:5-6). Don't lose everything for a passing pleasure. God warned Israel that they would receive, "the fruit of their thoughts," which they eventually did (Jer. 6:19).

WORSHIP AND PRAISE

People today love to talk about love, peace and cheap grace. . . [but] the zenith of praise and the highest form of worship are always connected with the holiness and glory of God.

The seraphim used their third pair of wings to fly. As they flew, they worshipped, exulting, "Holy, holy, holy is the LORD of Hosts; the whole earth is full of His glory" (Isa. 6:3). They flew and sang. That was worship on a very high scale indeed! The beat of their wings was music.

People today love to talk about love, peace and cheap grace; not much is mentioned about holiness. But isn't it amazing that these heavenly beings didn't cry, "Love, love, love," or "Peace, peace, peace," but a triune "Holy, holy, holy is the LORD of hosts." The zenith of praise and the highest form of worship are always connected with the holiness and glory of God.

How could these angels say that the whole earth is full of God's glory? Had they lived sheltered lives in the shadow of the Almighty? Had they never heard of heathen and atheistic empires, of war, hatred, greed and suffering? Yes, they had, but they saw them from a higher viewpoint as they flew before the throne. They had God's perspective, not the human view. Soaring above the earthly scene, the total situation revealed, they burst into rapturous exclamation. Scanning horizons beyond the sight of earth dwellers, the skies of all tomorrows, they sang, "the whole earth is full of His glory."

Get the Throne perspective. Believers are seated in heavenly places already in Christ Jesus (Eph. 2:6). What is your angle? Have you a molehill aspect or the Everest view? Are you a flatlander with a two-dimensional outlook, or are you a dweller on the spiritual highlands who has God's dimension added?

You ascend to God's Throne when you praise and worship. Praise lifts you. Doubt and murmuring, instead of wings of song, are boots of lead on your feet. In worship we contemplate the Throne, the power of the Lord, and His holiness. There we rest under His protection.

In the Throne room Isaiah was equipped, sent and cleansed with the altar fire in order to be God's servant with perfect integrity. Oh, glory to God! When we serve the Lord with purity of motive, rejoicing in His presence before His Throne, we are invincible, impregnable. Trouble starts when we lose the Throne perspective. But, elevated by worship to the Third Dimension, our character will be armor-plated.

THE SECOND KEY—AN EARTHLY EXAMPLE

I am writing out the following Scripture to be sure you will read it. Ponder it carefully and reverently. Let the Holy Spirit burn it into your soul.

> Here I am. Witness against me before the LORD and before His anointed: Whose ox have I taken, or whose donkey have I taken, or whom have I cheated? Whom have I oppressed, or from whose hand have I received any bribe with which to blind my eyes? I will restore it to you." (1 Sam. 12:3)

This bold challenge was part of the farewell speech of Samuel before Israel. The Judges Period of Israel ended with Samuel, who was by far the finest of these charismatic deliverers. His words, which I have quoted here, are amazing. In those early days, petty oppressions were regarded simply as a ruler's perks, and sheer tyranny surprised no one. For Samuel to be able to make a public challenge of his own integrity gives him a stature unequaled among the world's leaders.

Samuel's duty to govern and to deal with wrongdoers was absolute, and his judgments were without appeal. Those upon whom he had imposed penalties could have held a grudge against him and been very vindictive. His public words would have given them their opportunity. They could have spoken and claimed that he had done them ill.

SAMUEL: A PROTOTYPE TO FOLLOW

So, what happened? Samuel's reputation was so high that he had no fear. The massed representatives of the nation roared out, "You have not cheated us or oppressed us, nor have you taken anything from any man's hand." He had judged all, and now all judged him innocent, an unflawed man of God. A genuine prototype to follow.

Samuel had never taken a bribe or advantage on one single occasion for a period of a half century or more. Such remarkable behavior did not come only from being scrupulously thoughtful. In the heat of the moment, such restraint is not always possible. His heart was right, and that was his secret. Honesty had become his natural instinct as a man filled with God and with God's Word. Even when under pressure, with no time to consider, he instinctively knew "the right thing to do."

But the unanimous testimony of Israel was not enough for Samuel. He knew that people, sometimes all the people, can be fooled. For Samuel, only one judgment really mattered—the Lord's. We read, "So Samuel called to the LORD, and the LORD sent thunder and rain that day; and all the people greatly feared the LORD and Samuel" (1 Sam. 12:18).

God thundered His endorsement of His servant! It was harvest time, the dry season. But when the Lord's anointed prophet raised his arms and asked for heaven's vote, a miracle happened. The sky quickly filled with clouds and then came lightning, thunder and rain. This was God's "Amen" approving Samuel's integrity.

The people crouched in awe before such a supernatural display. God had exposed the heart of Samuel to them all. In all the humdrum, everyday duties of the people, Samuel had always acted with rectitude.

In his handling of money and every small judgment and decision, when nobody would have seen, God was still the observer of all. There had never been a bad or rotten deal.

Now God brought it to light and sealed it. Moreover, God gave a revelation of what it meant. He was with Samuel, and He and this man were as one. Samuel had a greatness with the greatness of the Lord, so that the very heavens responded to testify. Shady dealings, along with petty and sordid tricks, had no place in Samuel's record. Samuel's honesty linked him with the authority of God. An Israelite indeed in whom there was no guile!

When the Lord's anointed prophet raised his arms and asked for heaven's vote, a miracle happened. The sky quickly filled with clouds and then came lightning, thunder and rain. This was God's "Amen" approving Samuel's integrity.

That which is impure and shabby puts us outside the realm of the Spirit. God Himself will approve us when we keep both feet within the Kingdom of God. Power, glory and blessing will show earthly desire to be a murky shadow. The Almighty Himself embraces the cause of a man who can stand up and declare his integrity before the whole world, unafraid to ask "The Samuel Questions." The time to begin these godly practices is right now, at the beginning of one's ministry, not after having learned these truths by bitter experience. Even if you have sinned, you can truly repent and begin living in integrity now.

THE THIRD KEY—ANOINTED FOOTSTEPS

It is like the precious oil upon the head, running down on the beard, the beard of Aaron, running down on the edge of his garments. (Ps. 133:2)

What an anointing—so copious! That sacred oil flowed down his robes and dripped onto his feet and onto the floor. The ointment was specially prepared for the High Priest alone, and it carried its own unique perfume. Wherever Aaron walked, the oil on his feet and that which still dripped from the edges of his garments marked his movements. People could recognize his footsteps as those of the High Priest.

> *The memories of integrity in a man of God are better than an inscription on finest marble.*

May God grant that, even after we have left this world, we shall leave behind anointed footsteps for generations to come. The anointing of God upon you gives you the walk of Aaron. The memories of integrity in a man of God are better than an inscription on finest marble. Anointed men and women make history, which is everlasting in the kingdom of God.

Chapter 20

INTERCESSION-THE DETONATOR

*Evangelism without intercession is an explosive without
a detonator. Intercession without evangelism is a
detonator without an explosive.*

LEARNING FROM THE MEDIATOR
HOW TO BE INTERMEDIARIES

John Wesley noted, "God does everything by prayer and
nothing without it." In the New Testament alone there are 217
explicit references to prayer. Prayer brings oxygen to the
bloodstream of faith. Looking up to God, we don't go down.
God hears us all.

Jesus prayed. That seems natural enough, but upon
consideration, it is startling. In John 1:1-2 twice we read: "the
Word was with God." "With" here means "face to face," the
Father and the Son everlastingly in touch, nothing interrupting.
So why did Jesus ever pray? The answer is certainly not to set
up fellowship with God. It was because he *had* fellowship.
Prayer is as natural to fellowship as conversation between
children and parents. Why have fellowship and maintain
silence? The greater the saint, the more he will want to pray.

However, for Jesus it was more than indulgence in sweet
communion. He was an intercessor—*The Intercessor*. We will
look into that great intercessory prayer of Christ in John 17 and
learn from the Mediator Himself, how to be intermediaries.
Prayer is not primarily, "Give me!" "The Christian church is
the only organization on earth that exists for non-members,"
someone said. Its responsibilities include evangelism and
intercession.

A fact we need to face is that Jesus didn't just pray, He
preached. After intercession comes action. "Spiritual warfare"

> *Evangelism is essential to "spiritual warfare." Casting out Satan is a victory thrown away unless followed up by a wholesale Gospel assault. Otherwise Satan will reoccupy the position.*

for Him began as soon as the Holy Spirit came upon Him. He was led into the wilderness where He had a personal confrontation and duel with Satan himself. Afterward, He didn't just go home. He declared: "The Spirit of the LORD is upon Me, because He has anointed Me to preach the gospel" (Luke 4:18).

Prayer is one plan in God's grand strategy. Evangelism is essential to "spiritual warfare." Casting out Satan is a victory thrown away unless followed up by a wholesale Gospel assault. Otherwise Satan will reoccupy the position (Luke 11:26). Faith works for workers. Jesus said, "Pray!, Go!" *Pray* for laborers. *Go* as a laborer.

The Gospel is an explosive force but needs the detonator of prayer. Prayer however, has nothing to detonate without the preached Gospel. The Good News can't be news at all if it is not announced.

That is the outline of the divine strategy. First, the prayer bombardment against the entrenchment of the enemy. Then the infantry go in—the Gospel-witness battalions with the Word of God in hand—to take captives and occupy the position. At Jericho, Joshua did more than march and shout until Jericho's walls collapsed. His troops swarmed over and into the city, house to house, room to room, and consolidated Israel's possession.

Paul spoke of "the weapons of righteousness in the right hand and in the left" (2 Corinthians 6:7, NIV). From accounts of Roman military methods we know Paul observed the foot-soldier carrying his shield in his left hand and a short sword in his right hand for close combat. In Ephesians 6:16-17, he pictures the shield as faith-prayer and the sword as the Word of God,—essential equipment.

Scripture has a dozen different Greek words for prayer, but surprisingly, in referring to Jesus, John's Gospel does not use one of them. Jesus, John writes, just *"spoke"* to His Father, lifting up His eyes. For Him prayer was not a formal discipline, but His customary communication with the Father, anytime, anywhere.

When overpressed with the demands of the public, He went off somewhere quiet, (Luke 5:16). The KJV translation says, "He withdrew himself into the wilderness, and prayed." The NIV correctly puts it, "Jesus often withdrew to lonely places and prayed."

His own exclusive and unique approach to God created a new approach for us. "Learn from Me," Jesus said in Matthew 11:29. It is human instinct to pray. It is also human instinct to talk, but language is learned as children grow. Christian prayer is a language that needs to be learned as we grow in grace. It is quite striking that the disciples said to Jesus: "Lord, teach us to pray" (Luke 11:1), since they were Israelites and not ignorant of prayer. But watching Jesus they recognized something different.

The lesson we are interested in here is seeing Him as the Intercessor.

THE TRUE "LORD'S PRAYER"
John, Chapter 17

Although His relationship to the Father was on a higher level, Christ's prayers are our guide. Our great example is John 17, known as Christ's High Priestly Prayer. It is an outpouring of His deepest desires, very special and sacred; the words like "settings of silver" found to contain "apples of gold"— enriching truths, when opened up (Prov. 25:11).

1. As a preamble, we are struck by one repeated word on the lips of Jesus, the word: "World."

From Genesis to Malachi there are only words for the created "heaven and earth," the geographical world. These are used over 2,000 times in the Old Testament, and a few times in the New Testament, such as the "Roman World."

The word Jesus used is different—"kosmos." It is found 185 times in the New Testament, mostly in the Gospel and the letters of John (102 times), and in Paul's letters (47 times). English uses "cosmos" to mean only the material universe.

In the New Testament, "cosmos" is generally a special concept, the earthly scene of insurrection led by a usurping power (Ephesians 2:1-3). "The whole world lies under the sway of the wicked one" (1 John 5:19). The "world" is where the principle of sin operates, infecting everything. It is the world which Jesus referred to when He said, "My kingdom is not of this world. If My kingdom were of this world, My servants would fight," (John 18:36). The world is identified by its clash of arms. A greater feature now marks it. It is the world God so loved. All He had, He gave for all there was.

In this prayer Christ speaks of "world" in the material sense only once, (v.5) and 14 times of the enemy world of people, the area of His concern. Equally, or even more, He expressed concern for His disciples: "As You sent Me into the world, I also have sent them into the world" (v.18). They were not sent as secret fugitives to hide until God rescued them. They—we, have a bold and dynamic role as ambassadors with full authority from the King challenging the present rebellious order: "Be reconciled to God," (2 Cor. 5:20). "I pray . . . for those who will believe in Me through their message," (v.20). Hallelujah!

He said to His Father, "But now I come to you," (v.13). Then He adds, "I do not pray that You should take them out of the world," (v.15). He was going, but He asked that His disciples would be left here and not raptured yet. Jesus was not abandoning the world or the disciples. They would take His place. They were only a handful, but by them He would continue His love for the prodigal planet. He would leave them (and us) here until His consuming passion would be satisfied, heaven populated and hell left plundered. Jesus is not a stranger in this world. He is the Friend many have not yet met.

By our prayers God brings things about that He would not do without prayer. It is not a matter of changing God's will but of praying that His will shall be done.

Jesus inspired the apostles with a *world vision*. He is the "Savior of the world," not the Savior for a sprinkling of individuals (John 4:42). No one should think that in Christ they are too little to encompass entire continents with supplications. He is not the God of a cult, but "the God of the whole earth" (Isa. 54:5).

2. Christ prayed so that we would know how to pray.

What is prayer? Making requests to God seems to some people to be illogical. They say "You can't change the will of God. Prayer changes yourself. Prayer is really just meditation."

Well, Jesus prayed to God to change things and taught us to do the same. By our prayers God brings things about that He would not do without prayer. It is not a matter of changing God's will but of praying that His will shall be done (Matthew 6:10; 26:39). The possibility is that God's will may otherwise not be done. For instance, Jesus prayed for the disciples asking, in so many words, "they are yours, keep them." One would suppose that God would keep what was His anyway, but Jesus thought it proper to ask God to do so.

Prayer is not just as an exercise to sort yourself out, or to calm yourself down.   That would only be autosuggestion, psychology, or introspection—the thing James 1:24 describes as, "like a man observing his natural face in a mirror."

In this prayer Jesus says: "I have given them the words which You have given Me;" (v.8). Meditating on Scripture is always contemplating the Word of God. Concerning prayer Jesus said, "If . . . My words abide in you, you will ask what you desire, and it shall be done for you" (John 15:7). Something, usually anything, will soon fill an empty mind. Our mind should be filled with positive truth on which to meditate (Psalm 1). The fundamental idea is man speaking to God. God speaking to man generally is by His Spirit, through His Word.

3. Christ's prayer was intercessory.

"The Lord's prayer" as we call it, and this John 17 "Prayer of the Lord" are both filled with petitions. He poured out His soul for others. Individuals call it The Lord's Prayer but it begins "Our Father," and contains no personal requests.

Intercession is a passionate and vigorous activity, far removed from the recital of mere religious routine.   The Christian faith has been systematized. It has become gradually overlaid by traditions, sacred only because old, layer upon layer, like the centuries of varnish darkening the original color of brilliant masterpieces.   Christ laid down no system of observances and invocations. He came to bring life and energy, and no formality could possibly tap the divine resources. The cross and empty tomb are the twin towers of the world's greatest power plant.

No world-religion has an exhortation like Matthew 7:7-11, or a prayer like John 17. One Greek word occurs there 19 times, "hina" meaning "so that." Jesus prayed *so that* things would be done. Some people pray five times daily asking for nothing. They say, blessed is he who asks for nothing for he shall not be disappointed! Tibetans endlessly repeat, "O the jewel on the lotus bud"; Yoga gurus mutter a single word mantra; and the Moslem dies with no appeal on his lips except, "God is one, Allah is his name and Muhammad is his prophet." One and all bow to the inscrutable will of whatever Fates they think exist. Allah, Buddha and Krishna are not remotely like the God and Father of our Lord Jesus Christ. They bring no salvation, no miracles, no forgiveness, no peace, no power, no help.

4. The prayers of Jesus were outbursts to God.

Jesus prayed with "strong crying and tears" (Heb. 5:7), and sweated "as it were great drops of blood falling down to the ground" (Luke 22:44).

Bible words describing prayer have roots in shouting. Prayer is an outcry. People in Bible days didn't have a "quiet time." They "called on God," and "cried unto Him," putting everything into it.

He and the apostles taught us that we must expect prayer to be answered. We are not to be apologetic or vague—"not doubting" as James puts it (James 1:6). Prayer is not a pious collection of good wishes, nervous hints or hopes. It is the *"effective, fervent prayer of a righteous man"* (James 5:16), that sees things happen. Jesus at the tomb of Lazarus showed signs of tremendous inner disturbance, "He groaned in the spirit and was troubled" and, "Jesus wept" (John 11:33,35).

Bible words describing prayer have roots in shouting. Prayer is an outcry. When Hannah prayed, moving only her lips, they thought she was drunk (1 Sam. 1:13-14). People in Bible days didn't have a "quiet time"— they "called on God," and "cried unto Him," putting everything into it. Ezra for example, said, "I fell on my knees and spread out my hands to

That's the real basis for fasting, throwing ourselves into the business of intercession, an articulation of God-inspired desire. Otherwise it is just a hunger strike.

the LORD my God." Ezra was "confessing, weeping and bowing down before the house of God." (Ezra 9:5;10:1). Daniel prayed loud enough to be heard outside his house by his enemies (Dan.6:10-11). He did not mutter.

It is not just the loudness but it is the passion and compassion which prompts prayer. If we hate people being sick, or have a revulsion for the presence of foul spirits—the work of the enemy, is it possible for us to coo like a dove? Hasn't righteous indignation some justification for vehemence against the works of hell?

Bawling through a high-powered microphone will not scare even the most nervous demon. Nor will fasting—unless our hunger for God becomes greater than our hunger for food. But the devil doesn't like the fact that we get so mad at him we put off everything, even meals. That's the real basis for fasting, throwing ourselves into the business of intercession, an articulation of God-inspired desire. Otherwise it is just a hunger strike. I never knew that I would be able to fast for long, but then I had such a God-given, burning desire to do it, that forty days just slipped by. I am sure, that the weight my body lost, my spirit gained: God was in action in my ministry.

Fasting may be more than fasting from food. Isaiah and Jeremiah say the fast God wants is fasting from sin. If Christians, weeping before God, gave up their self-indulgent habits and resolved to leave alone their greed, or their jealousy, gossiping, pride or uncleanness, for even a week, it would be far more effective than missing dinner every night.

Prayer, with or without fasting, has to be "fervent," not coming to God casually, "pushing the door open with a careless shoulder," as somebody said, hand in pockets with a familiar, "Hello God!" attitude. When the early church gathered, they "raised their voice to God with one accord" in prayer. After they had prayed, "the place where they were assembled together was shaken; and they were all filled with the Holy Spirit, and they spoke the word of God with boldness" (Acts 4:24-31). That's praying! And preaching!

That is also the praying-power behind our CfaN crusades— vocal, noisy perhaps, but over the top for God. People complain about "noisy Charismatics" and say God isn't deaf— (He isn't nervous either!)—and that Jesus healed the sick quietly. True maybe, but Jesus also shouted "with a loud voice." God expects us to make it a robust business when we come to Him.

As for me, when they were sick, my clothing was sackcloth: I humbled my soul with fasting. . . . I behaved as though he had been my friend or brother; I bowed down heavily, as one that mourneth for his mother." (Psalm 35:13-14 KJV)

The matters that Scripture puts before us to pray about are not casual conveniences like what to eat, drink or wear, or where to find the right color neckwear. Jesus prayed, "Holy Father, protect them by the power of your Name" (John 17:11 NIV). Paul exhorts similarly in Romans 15:30-33. We are to pray for and expect forgiveness for ourselves (Matthew 6:12); for the forgiveness and deliverance of others—both sinners and the saved (1 John 5:16, James 5:15-16); for laborers to be sent into the harvest (Matt. 9:38); for the Gifts of the Spirit (1 Cor. 14:1); and for God's name to be honored. We are to also pray for His will to be done and His Kingdom to come, for ourselves in trial, for people to be healed, for those with burdens, for kings and rulers, for the unity of God's people and the many other concerns of the Kingdom of God shown in the Scriptures.

These are needs, not preferences, mostly centering on the needs of others and the salvation of souls. Jesus prayed saying: "I pray also for those who will believe in Me through their message" (John 7:20 NIV). What Jesus said here is expanded later by Paul in First Timothy 2:1-4:

> Therefore I exhort first of all that supplications, prayers, intercessions, and giving of thanks be made for all men, for kings and all who are in authority. . . . For this is good and acceptable in the sight of God our Savior, who desires all men to be saved and to come to the knowledge of the truth.

If we are to pray that, it is obviously God's will to save people and we are to pray for the will of God to be done. It includes everything that goes into saving people—the entire work of evangelism, and for converts to be "kept from the evil one," as Jesus prayed. Notice the tremendous surge of feelings in Paul's heart:

> Now I beg you, brethren, through the Lord Jesus Christ, and through the love of the Spirit, that you strive together with me in prayers to God for me that I may be delivered from those . . . who do not believe. (Rom. 15:30-31)

> Praying always with all prayer and supplication in the Spirit, being watchful to this end with all perseverance and supplication for all the saints—and for me, that utterance may be given to me, that I may open my mouth boldly to make known the mystery of the gospel. (Eph. 6:18-19)

5. Jesus prayed in terms of complete assurance of God, and repeatedly used the word "know."

He said, "I have given them Your word" (v.14), and that word stresses over and over again that God *always* hears prayer.

when we pray according to His will. And to pray according to His will means to pray in line with the Word of God.

Praying is not futile when we know Him. The Bible hammers this fact home, blow after blow. The following is a continuous paragraph of assurances from the New Testament alone:

[1]Your Father knows what you need before you ask him. [2]Ask and it will be given to you. Everyone who asks receives. How much more will your Father in heaven give good gifts to those who ask him! [3]Again, I tell you that if two of you on earth agree about anything you ask for, it will be done for you by my Father in heaven. [4]If you believe, you will receive whatever you ask for in prayer. [5]And I will do whatever you ask in my name, so that the Son may bring glory to the Father. [6]If you remain in me and my words remain in you, ask whatever you wish, and it will be given you. [7]I tell you the truth, my Father will give you whatever you ask in my name. [8]If any of you lacks wisdom, he should ask God, who gives generously to all without finding fault, and it will be given to him. [9]If our hearts do not condemn us, we have confidence before God and receive from him anything we ask, because we obey his commands and do what pleases him. [10]This is the confidence we have in approaching God: that if we ask anything according to his will, he hears us. And if we know that he hears us—whatever we ask—we know that we have what we asked of him.

[1]Matt.6:8; [2]Matt. 7:7-11; [3]Matt. 18:19; [4]Matt 21:22; [5]John 14:13; [6]John 15:7; [7]John 16:23; [8]James 1:5; [9]1John 3:21-22; [10]1John 5:14-15; NIV

6. Jesus said: "Sanctify them by your truth. Your word is truth." John 17:17

Some suppose that effective praying awaits our Christian sanctification. That can be left to the Lord who is our sanctifier. It is the easiest thing in the world to discover how human people are and "why revival tarries." We are, however, sons, whatever our shortcomings. God hears us because we are sons. He does not look for what we've done but what we *are*—in Him, sanctified in His sight, and to be heard.

7. Jesus spoke of "The power of Your name, the name You gave Me." John 17:11 (NIV)

Therein lies the dawn of a new age. Christ taught us to pray "in His name." Before His name was given, people presented themselves to God as themselves, as we see in the Psalms.

Reading the prayers of great figures like Ezra and Daniel, Elijah and Moses, the credentials they presented were completely different. They came as themselves. But we come in Christ. Christ came to the Father in His own Name, and we stand with Him in His name, not claiming the rights of law, our race, or our goodness. The Psalmist came before God with this kind of appeal:

"I do not sit with deceitful men, nor do I consort with hypocrites. . . . I wash my hands in innocence, and go about your altar, O LORD." (Psalm 26: 4-6 NIV)

To be heard, these men "brought forth their strong reasons," that they belonged to God's covenant people, they quoted His past miracles, or challenged Him to maintain His honor—all legitimate pleas even now. But the Christian approach is "a new and living way,"—His Name—the name of Jesus, the name that the Father gave Him. The One in whom we stand cannot be faulted. "I in them, and You in Me; that they may be made perfect in one" (John 17:23).

In Christ, the least distinguished people carry Kingdom status, though not for the indulgence of personal fancies. When Jesus spoke of food, drink and dress he implied that God needed no reminding about these things. Our aims should concentrate on "the kingdom of God" (Matt. 6:26-34). "The Lord's prayer" contains various petitions but they all are facets of the one central and key request: *"thy Kingdom come."*

It would be quite impossible for the Bible to list every request permitted. But they all focus on the same word "thy Kingdom come," the work of salvation. Look at what Scripture says about "groaning." Romans 8:26: "We do not know what we should pray for, . . . but the Spirit

> *In Christ the least distinguished people carry Kingdom status.*

Himself makes intercession for us with groanings which cannot be uttered." The same groaning again in verse 22, when the redemption of the whole world is in view, and again in verse 23, "we ourselves groan within ourselves, eagerly waiting . . . redemption." That redemption involves creation itself.

The burden of a world lost in wickedness lies heavily upon the heart of God. Christ groaned, creation groans, sinners groan, believers groan, and the Spirit groans on behalf of all. Then His groans are prayers, translated into eloquence by God for the hope of mankind. It is when we intercede with desires for the lost world that the Spirit "helps us in our weakness", and our "groans" become levers to move mountains.

Some competent scholars consider that by "groans" Paul includes tongues-speaking. When the burden is heavy, hand it over to the Holy Spirit and let Him pray through us in those "groanings" of His.

In John 11:33-43, we read that Lazarus had died. When Jesus came, "He groaned in the spirit and was troubled," (a very strong expression), and, "Jesus wept" (v.35). Then in verses 41-42, Jesus prayed, "Father, I thank You that You have heard Me. And I know that You always hear Me." Notice that Jesus had said no prayer at all; He had only groaned and wept. Jesus was groaning not because of Lazarus only, but for the whole world, and the sorrows and fear of death which haunted the human race. He carried that sorrow in His soul to Calvary, and there "tasted death for every man." Jesus the Intercessor put His very life into it.

8. Jesus said: "That the world may know that You have sent Me." John 17:23

This prayer is in harmony with His command to us to "teach all nations." Any Christian who loses that perspective is short sighted. We read that in the beginning, "the earth was without form and void; and darkness was on the face of the deep. And the Spirit of God was hovering over the face of the waters" (Gen. 1:2). Today God's Spirit broods over the spiritual darkness of our sinful world. He "groans"— but now He has allies. He utters His creative concern through the newborn children of God. He intercedes and puts that ministry upon us, the same ministry as the Son of God in glory who also intercedes.

In our ministry (CfaN), we are taking intercession very seriously and pair it with the anointed preaching of the Gospel of Jesus Christ. Our intercessors are the Detonators that bring down the walls of Satan's stronghold. The results of our Gospel crusades in Africa are awesome. Within the twelve month period of crusades from mid-1991 to mid-1992, we preached face to face to a total of over eight million people in Africa alone, and of these two million responded to the call of salvation. Signs and wonders follow the preaching of the Word of God. The combination of this kind of intercession and power-evangelism leaves Satan absolutely helpless and brings about the revival which is conquering the world.

6 inspirational teaching audio tapes by Reinhard Bonnke

- How to receive a miracle
- The harvest is ripe
- Arrows of deliverance
- How to launch a life with God
- Listening to the call
- God's last word

Now you can enjoy this entire teaching set
for the **special price of only $19.99**.

(Regular price $25.00. All prices excluding shipping and handling.)